C-1594  CAREER EXAMINATION SERIES

*This is your*
*PASSBOOK for...*

# Senior Probation Officer

*Test Preparation Study Guide*
*Questions & Answers*

# COPYRIGHT NOTICE

This book is SOLELY intended for, is sold ONLY to, and its use is RESTRICTED to individual, bona fide applicants or candidates who qualify by virtue of having seriously filed applications for appropriate license, certificate, professional and/or promotional advancement, higher school matriculation, scholarship, or other legitimate requirements of education and/or governmental authorities.

This book is NOT intended for use, class instruction, tutoring, training, duplication, copying, reprinting, excerption, or adaptation, etc., by:

1) Other publishers
2) Proprietors and/or Instructors of "Coaching" and/or Preparatory Courses
3) Personnel and/or Training Divisions of commercial, industrial, and governmental organizations
4) Schools, colleges, or universities and/or their departments and staffs, including teachers and other personnel
5) Testing Agencies or Bureaus
6) Study groups which seek by the purchase of a single volume to copy and/or duplicate and/or adapt this material for use by the group as a whole without having purchased individual volumes for each of the members of the group
7) Et al.

Such persons would be in violation of appropriate Federal and State statutes.

PROVISION OF LICENSING AGREEMENTS – Recognized educational, commercial, industrial, and governmental institutions and organizations, and others legitimately engaged in educational pursuits, including training, testing, and measurement activities, may address request for a licensing agreement to the copyright owners, who will determine whether, and under what conditions, including fees and charges, the materials in this book may be used them.  In other words, a licensing facility exists for the legitimate use of the material in this book on other than an individual basis.  However, it is asseverated and affirmed here that the material in this book CANNOT be used without the receipt of the express permission of such a licensing agreement from the Publishers. Inquiries re licensing should be addressed to the company, attention rights and permissions department.

All rights reserved, including the right of reproduction in whole or in part, in any form or by any means, electronic or mechanical, including photocopying, recording, or by any information storage and retrieval system, without permission in writing from the Publisher.

Copyright © 2024 by
## National Learning Corporation

212 Michael Drive, Syosset, NY 11791
(516) 921-8888 • www.passbooks.com
E-mail: info@passbooks.com

# PASSBOOK® SERIES

THE *PASSBOOK® SERIES* has been created to prepare applicants and candidates for the ultimate academic battlefield – the examination room.

At some time in our lives, each and every one of us may be required to take an examination – for validation, matriculation, admission, qualification, registration, certification, or licensure.

Based on the assumption that every applicant or candidate has met the basic formal educational standards, has taken the required number of courses, and read the necessary texts, the *PASSBOOK® SERIES* furnishes the one special preparation which may assure passing with confidence, instead of failing with insecurity. Examination questions – together with answers – are furnished as the basic vehicle for study so that the mysteries of the examination and its compounding difficulties may be eliminated or diminished by a sure method.

This book is meant to help you pass your examination provided that you qualify and are serious in your objective.

The entire field is reviewed through the huge store of content information which is succinctly presented through a provocative and challenging approach – the question-and-answer method.

A climate of success is established by furnishing the correct answers at the end of each test.

You soon learn to recognize types of questions, forms of questions, and patterns of questioning. You may even begin to anticipate expected outcomes.

You perceive that many questions are repeated or adapted so that you can gain acute insights, which may enable you to score many sure points.

You learn how to confront new questions, or types of questions, and to attack them confidently and work out the correct answers.

You note objectives and emphases, and recognize pitfalls and dangers, so that you may make positive educational adjustments.

Moreover, you are kept fully informed in relation to new concepts, methods, practices, and directions in the field.

You discover that you are actually taking the examination all the time: you are preparing for the examination by "taking" an examination, not by reading extraneous and/or supererogatory textbooks.

In short, this PASSBOOK®, used directedly, should be an important factor in helping you to pass your test.

# SENIOR PROBATION OFFICER

DUTIES
An employee in this class performs professional probation work as a specialist in one of several areas including warrant and arrest procedures, violent crimes, alcohol and drug dependency, internal affairs and sex crimes. The incumbent performs intake, investigations, group treatment and other functions with a specialized client base. The incumbent does not have direct supervisory responsibility, but may direct and train probation staff assigned to the specialty unit as assistants handling the less complex cases and issues. Work is performed under the general supervision of a Supervising Probation Officer, and is reviewed through conferences and written reports. Does related work as required.

SCOPE OF THE EXAMINATION
The written test will cover knowledge, skills and/or abilities in such areas as:

1. Educating and interacting with the public;
2. Establishing and maintaining working relationships with defendants/respondents and probationers;
3. Preparing written material; and
4. Probation casework, including trends and developments in probation programs and services.

# HOW TO TAKE A TEST

I. YOU MUST PASS AN EXAMINATION

A. *WHAT EVERY CANDIDATE SHOULD KNOW*

Examination applicants often ask us for help in preparing for the written test. What can I study in advance? What kinds of questions will be asked? How will the test be given? How will the papers be graded?

As an applicant for a civil service examination, you may be wondering about some of these things. Our purpose here is to suggest effective methods of advance study and to describe civil service examinations.

Your chances for success on this examination can be increased if you know how to prepare. Those "pre-examination jitters" can be reduced if you know what to expect. You can even experience an adventure in good citizenship if you know why civil service exams are given.

B. *WHY ARE CIVIL SERVICE EXAMINATIONS GIVEN?*

Civil service examinations are important to you in two ways. As a citizen, you want public jobs filled by employees who know how to do their work. As a job seeker, you want a fair chance to compete for that job on an equal footing with other candidates. The best-known means of accomplishing this two-fold goal is the competitive examination.

Exams are widely publicized throughout the nation. They may be administered for jobs in federal, state, city, municipal, town or village governments or agencies.

Any citizen may apply, with some limitations, such as the age or residence of applicants. Your experience and education may be reviewed to see whether you meet the requirements for the particular examination. When these requirements exist, they are reasonable and applied consistently to all applicants. Thus, a competitive examination may cause you some uneasiness now, but it is your privilege and safeguard.

C. *HOW ARE CIVIL SERVICE EXAMS DEVELOPED?*

Examinations are carefully written by trained technicians who are specialists in the field known as "psychological measurement," in consultation with recognized authorities in the field of work that the test will cover. These experts recommend the subject matter areas or skills to be tested; only those knowledges or skills important to your success on the job are included. The most reliable books and source materials available are used as references. Together, the experts and technicians judge the difficulty level of the questions.

Test technicians know how to phrase questions so that the problem is clearly stated. Their ethics do not permit "trick" or "catch" questions. Questions may have been tried out on sample groups, or subjected to statistical analysis, to determine their usefulness.

Written tests are often used in combination with performance tests, ratings of training and experience, and oral interviews. All of these measures combine to form the best-known means of finding the right person for the right job.

## II. HOW TO PASS THE WRITTEN TEST

### A. NATURE OF THE EXAMINATION

To prepare intelligently for civil service examinations, you should know how they differ from school examinations you have taken. In school you were assigned certain definite pages to read or subjects to cover. The examination questions were quite detailed and usually emphasized memory. Civil service exams, on the other hand, try to discover your present ability to perform the duties of a position, plus your potentiality to learn these duties. In other words, a civil service exam attempts to predict how successful you will be. Questions cover such a broad area that they cannot be as minute and detailed as school exam questions.

In the public service similar kinds of work, or positions, are grouped together in one "class." This process is known as *position-classification*. All the positions in a class are paid according to the salary range for that class. One class title covers all of these positions, and they are all tested by the same examination.

### B. FOUR BASIC STEPS

**1) Study the announcement**

How, then, can you know what subjects to study? Our best answer is: "Learn as much as possible about the class of positions for which you've applied." The exam will test the knowledge, skills and abilities needed to do the work.

Your most valuable source of information about the position you want is the official exam announcement. This announcement lists the training and experience qualifications. Check these standards and apply only if you come reasonably close to meeting them.

The brief description of the position in the examination announcement offers some clues to the subjects which will be tested. Think about the job itself. Review the duties in your mind. Can you perform them, or are there some in which you are rusty? Fill in the blank spots in your preparation.

Many jurisdictions preview the written test in the exam announcement by including a section called "Knowledge and Abilities Required," "Scope of the Examination," or some similar heading. Here you will find out specifically what fields will be tested.

**2) Review your own background**

Once you learn in general what the position is all about, and what you need to know to do the work, ask yourself which subjects you already know fairly well and which need improvement. You may wonder whether to concentrate on improving your strong areas or on building some background in your fields of weakness. When the announcement has specified "some knowledge" or "considerable knowledge," or has used adjectives like "beginning principles of..." or "advanced ... methods," you can get a clue as to the number and difficulty of questions to be asked in any given field. More questions, and hence broader coverage, would be included for those subjects which are more important in the work. Now weigh your strengths and weaknesses against the job requirements and prepare accordingly.

**3) Determine the level of the position**

Another way to tell how intensively you should prepare is to understand the level of the job for which you are applying. Is it the entering level? In other words, is this the position in which beginners in a field of work are hired? Or is it an intermediate or advanced level? Sometimes this is indicated by such words as "Junior" or "Senior" in the class title. Other jurisdictions use Roman numerals to designate the level – Clerk I, Clerk II, for example. The word "Supervisor" sometimes appears in the title. If the level is not indicated by the title, check the description of duties. Will you be working under very close supervision, or will you have responsibility for independent decisions in this work?

### 4) Choose appropriate study materials

Now that you know the subjects to be examined and the relative amount of each subject to be covered, you can choose suitable study materials. For beginning level jobs, or even advanced ones, if you have a pronounced weakness in some aspect of your training, read a modern, standard textbook in that field. Be sure it is up to date and has general coverage. Such books are normally available at your library, and the librarian will be glad to help you locate one. For entry-level positions, questions of appropriate difficulty are chosen – neither highly advanced questions, nor those too simple. Such questions require careful thought but not advanced training.

If the position for which you are applying is technical or advanced, you will read more advanced, specialized material. If you are already familiar with the basic principles of your field, elementary textbooks would waste your time. Concentrate on advanced textbooks and technical periodicals. Think through the concepts and review difficult problems in your field.

These are all general sources. You can get more ideas on your own initiative, following these leads. For example, training manuals and publications of the government agency which employs workers in your field can be useful, particularly for technical and professional positions. A letter or visit to the government department involved may result in more specific study suggestions, and certainly will provide you with a more definite idea of the exact nature of the position you are seeking.

## III. KINDS OF TESTS

Tests are used for purposes other than measuring knowledge and ability to perform specified duties. For some positions, it is equally important to test ability to make adjustments to new situations or to profit from training. In others, basic mental abilities not dependent on information are essential. Questions which test these things may not appear as pertinent to the duties of the position as those which test for knowledge and information. Yet they are often highly important parts of a fair examination. For very general questions, it is almost impossible to help you direct your study efforts. What we can do is to point out some of the more common of these general abilities needed in public service positions and describe some typical questions.

1) General information

Broad, general information has been found useful for predicting job success in some kinds of work. This is tested in a variety of ways, from vocabulary lists to questions about current events. Basic background in some field of work, such as sociology or economics, may be sampled in a group of questions. Often these are principles which have become familiar to most persons through exposure rather than through formal training. It is difficult to advise you how to study for these questions; being alert to the world around you is our best suggestion.

2) Verbal ability

An example of an ability needed in many positions is verbal or language ability. Verbal ability is, in brief, the ability to use and understand words. Vocabulary and grammar tests are typical measures of this ability. Reading comprehension or paragraph interpretation questions are common in many kinds of civil service tests. You are given a paragraph of written material and asked to find its central meaning.

3) Numerical ability

Number skills can be tested by the familiar arithmetic problem, by checking paired lists of numbers to see which are alike and which are different, or by interpreting charts and graphs. In the latter test, a graph may be printed in the test booklet which you are asked to use as the basis for answering questions.

4) Observation

A popular test for law-enforcement positions is the observation test. A picture is shown to you for several minutes, then taken away. Questions about the picture test your ability to observe both details and larger elements.

5) Following directions

In many positions in the public service, the employee must be able to carry out written instructions dependably and accurately. You may be given a chart with several columns, each column listing a variety of information. The questions require you to carry out directions involving the information given in the chart.

6) Skills and aptitudes

Performance tests effectively measure some manual skills and aptitudes. When the skill is one in which you are trained, such as typing or shorthand, you can practice. These tests are often very much like those given in business school or high school courses. For many of the other skills and aptitudes, however, no short-time preparation can be made. Skills and abilities natural to you or that you have developed throughout your lifetime are being tested.

Many of the general questions just described provide all the data needed to answer the questions and ask you to use your reasoning ability to find the answers. Your best preparation for these tests, as well as for tests of facts and ideas, is to be at your physical and mental best. You, no doubt, have your own methods of getting into an exam-taking mood and keeping "in shape." The next section lists some ideas on this subject.

IV. KINDS OF QUESTIONS

Only rarely is the "essay" question, which you answer in narrative form, used in civil service tests. Civil service tests are usually of the short-answer type. Full instructions for answering these questions will be given to you at the examination. But in case this is your first experience with short-answer questions and separate answer sheets, here is what you need to know:

**1) Multiple-choice Questions**

Most popular of the short-answer questions is the "multiple choice" or "best answer" question. It can be used, for example, to test for factual knowledge, ability to solve problems or judgment in meeting situations found at work.

A multiple-choice question is normally one of three types—
- It can begin with an incomplete statement followed by several possible endings. You are to find the one ending which *best* completes the statement, although some of the others may not be entirely wrong.
- It can also be a complete statement in the form of a question which is answered by choosing one of the statements listed.

- It can be in the form of a problem – again you select the best answer.

Here is an example of a multiple-choice question with a discussion which should give you some clues as to the method for choosing the right answer:

When an employee has a complaint about his assignment, the action which will *best* help him overcome his difficulty is to
   A. discuss his difficulty with his coworkers
   B. take the problem to the head of the organization
   C. take the problem to the person who gave him the assignment
   D. say nothing to anyone about his complaint

In answering this question, you should study each of the choices to find which is best. Consider choice "A" – Certainly an employee may discuss his complaint with fellow employees, but no change or improvement can result, and the complaint remains unresolved. Choice "B" is a poor choice since the head of the organization probably does not know what assignment you have been given, and taking your problem to him is known as "going over the head" of the supervisor. The supervisor, or person who made the assignment, is the person who can clarify it or correct any injustice. Choice "C" is, therefore, correct. To say nothing, as in choice "D," is unwise. Supervisors have and interest in knowing the problems employees are facing, and the employee is seeking a solution to his problem.

## 2) True/False Questions

The "true/false" or "right/wrong" form of question is sometimes used. Here a complete statement is given. Your job is to decide whether the statement is right or wrong.

SAMPLE: A roaming cell-phone call to a nearby city costs less than a non-roaming call to a distant city.

This statement is wrong, or false, since roaming calls are more expensive.
This is not a complete list of all possible question forms, although most of the others are variations of these common types. You will always get complete directions for answering questions. Be sure you understand *how* to mark your answers – ask questions until you do.

## V. RECORDING YOUR ANSWERS

Computer terminals are used more and more today for many different kinds of exams.
For an examination with very few applicants, you may be told to record your answers in the test booklet itself. Separate answer sheets are much more common. If this separate answer sheet is to be scored by machine – and this is often the case – it is highly important that you mark your answers correctly in order to get credit.
An electronic scoring machine is often used in civil service offices because of the speed with which papers can be scored. Machine-scored answer sheets must be marked with a pencil, which will be given to you. This pencil has a high graphite content which responds to the electronic scoring machine. As a matter of fact, stray dots may register as answers, so do not let your pencil rest on the answer sheet while you are pondering the correct answer. Also, if your pencil lead breaks or is otherwise defective, ask for another.

Since the answer sheet will be dropped in a slot in the scoring machine, be careful not to bend the corners or get the paper crumpled.

The answer sheet normally has five vertical columns of numbers, with 30 numbers to a column. These numbers correspond to the question numbers in your test booklet. After each number, going across the page are four or five pairs of dotted lines. These short dotted lines have small letters or numbers above them. The first two pairs may also have a "T" or "F" above the letters. This indicates that the first two pairs only are to be used if the questions are of the true-false type. If the questions are multiple choice, disregard the "T" and "F" and pay attention only to the small letters or numbers.

Answer your questions in the manner of the sample that follows:

    32. The largest city in the United States is
        A. Washington, D.C.
        B. New York City
        C. Chicago
        D. Detroit
        E. San Francisco

1) Choose the answer you think is best. (New York City is the largest, so "B" is correct.)
2) Find the row of dotted lines numbered the same as the question you are answering. (Find row number 32)
3) Find the pair of dotted lines corresponding to the answer. (Find the pair of lines under the mark "B.")
4) Make a solid black mark between the dotted lines.


## VI. BEFORE THE TEST

Common sense will help you find procedures to follow to get ready for an examination. Too many of us, however, overlook these sensible measures. Indeed, nervousness and fatigue have been found to be the most serious reasons why applicants fail to do their best on civil service tests. Here is a list of reminders:

- Begin your preparation early – Don't wait until the last minute to go scurrying around for books and materials or to find out what the position is all about.
- Prepare continuously – An hour a night for a week is better than an all-night cram session. This has been definitely established. What is more, a night a week for a month will return better dividends than crowding your study into a shorter period of time.
- Locate the place of the exam – You have been sent a notice telling you when and where to report for the examination. If the location is in a different town or otherwise unfamiliar to you, it would be well to inquire the best route and learn something about the building.
- Relax the night before the test – Allow your mind to rest. Do not study at all that night. Plan some mild recreation or diversion; then go to bed early and get a good night's sleep.
- Get up early enough to make a leisurely trip to the place for the test – This way unforeseen events, traffic snarls, unfamiliar buildings, etc. will not upset you.
- Dress comfortably – A written test is not a fashion show. You will be known by number and not by name, so wear something comfortable.

- Leave excess paraphernalia at home – Shopping bags and odd bundles will get in your way. You need bring only the items mentioned in the official notice you received; usually everything you need is provided. Do not bring reference books to the exam. They will only confuse those last minutes and be taken away from you when in the test room.
- Arrive somewhat ahead of time – If because of transportation schedules you must get there very early, bring a newspaper or magazine to take your mind off yourself while waiting.
- Locate the examination room – When you have found the proper room, you will be directed to the seat or part of the room where you will sit. Sometimes you are given a sheet of instructions to read while you are waiting. Do not fill out any forms until you are told to do so; just read them and be prepared.
- Relax and prepare to listen to the instructions
- If you have any physical problem that may keep you from doing your best, be sure to tell the test administrator. If you are sick or in poor health, you really cannot do your best on the exam. You can come back and take the test some other time.

## VII. AT THE TEST

The day of the test is here and you have the test booklet in your hand. The temptation to get going is very strong. Caution! There is more to success than knowing the right answers. You must know how to identify your papers and understand variations in the type of short-answer question used in this particular examination. Follow these suggestions for maximum results from your efforts:

### 1) Cooperate with the monitor

The test administrator has a duty to create a situation in which you can be as much at ease as possible. He will give instructions, tell you when to begin, check to see that you are marking your answer sheet correctly, and so on. He is not there to guard you, although he will see that your competitors do not take unfair advantage. He wants to help you do your best.

### 2) Listen to all instructions

Don't jump the gun! Wait until you understand all directions. In most civil service tests you get more time than you need to answer the questions. So don't be in a hurry. Read each word of instructions until you clearly understand the meaning. Study the examples, listen to all announcements and follow directions. Ask questions if you do not understand what to do.

### 3) Identify your papers

Civil service exams are usually identified by number only. You will be assigned a number; you must not put your name on your test papers. Be sure to copy your number correctly. Since more than one exam may be given, copy your exact examination title.

### 4) Plan your time

Unless you are told that a test is a "speed" or "rate of work" test, speed itself is usually not important. Time enough to answer all the questions will be provided, but this does not mean that you have all day. An overall time limit has been set. Divide the total time (in minutes) by the number of questions to determine the approximate time you have for each question.

### 5) Do not linger over difficult questions

If you come across a difficult question, mark it with a paper clip (useful to have along) and come back to it when you have been through the booklet. One caution if you do this – be sure to skip a number on your answer sheet as well. Check often to be sure that you have not lost your place and that you are marking in the row numbered the same as the question you are answering.

### 6) Read the questions

Be sure you know what the question asks! Many capable people are unsuccessful because they failed to *read* the questions correctly.

### 7) Answer all questions

Unless you have been instructed that a penalty will be deducted for incorrect answers, it is better to guess than to omit a question.

### 8) Speed tests

It is often better NOT to guess on speed tests. It has been found that on timed tests people are tempted to spend the last few seconds before time is called in marking answers at random – without even reading them – in the hope of picking up a few extra points. To discourage this practice, the instructions may warn you that your score will be "corrected" for guessing. That is, a penalty will be applied. The incorrect answers will be deducted from the correct ones, or some other penalty formula will be used.

### 9) Review your answers

If you finish before time is called, go back to the questions you guessed or omitted to give them further thought. Review other answers if you have time.

### 10) Return your test materials

If you are ready to leave before others have finished or time is called, take ALL your materials to the monitor and leave quietly. Never take any test material with you. The monitor can discover whose papers are not complete, and taking a test booklet may be grounds for disqualification.

## VIII. EXAMINATION TECHNIQUES

1) Read the general instructions carefully. These are usually printed on the first page of the exam booklet. As a rule, these instructions refer to the timing of the examination; the fact that you should not start work until the signal and must stop work at a signal, etc. If there are any *special* instructions, such as a choice of questions to be answered, make sure that you note this instruction carefully.

2) When you are ready to start work on the examination, that is as soon as the signal has been given, read the instructions to each question booklet, underline any key words or phrases, such as *least, best, outline, describe* and the like. In this way you will tend to answer as requested rather than discover on reviewing your paper that you *listed without describing*, that you selected the *worst* choice rather than the *best* choice, etc.

3) If the examination is of the objective or multiple-choice type – that is, each question will also give a series of possible answers: A, B, C or D, and you are called upon to select the best answer and write the letter next to that answer on your answer paper – it is advisable to start answering each question in turn. There may be anywhere from 50 to 100 such questions in the three or four hours allotted and you can see how much time would be taken if you read through all the questions before beginning to answer any. Furthermore, if you come across a question or group of questions which you know would be difficult to answer, it would undoubtedly affect your handling of all the other questions.

4) If the examination is of the essay type and contains but a few questions, it is a moot point as to whether you should read all the questions before starting to answer any one. Of course, if you are given a choice – say five out of seven and the like – then it is essential to read all the questions so you can eliminate the two that are most difficult. If, however, you are asked to answer all the questions, there may be danger in trying to answer the easiest one first because you may find that you will spend too much time on it. The best technique is to answer the first question, then proceed to the second, etc.

5) Time your answers. Before the exam begins, write down the time it started, then add the time allowed for the examination and write down the time it must be completed, then divide the time available somewhat as follows:
    - If 3-1/2 hours are allowed, that would be 210 minutes. If you have 80 objective-type questions, that would be an average of 2-1/2 minutes per question. Allow yourself no more than 2 minutes per question, or a total of 160 minutes, which will permit about 50 minutes to review.
    - If for the time allotment of 210 minutes there are 7 essay questions to answer, that would average about 30 minutes a question. Give yourself only 25 minutes per question so that you have about 35 minutes to review.

6) The most important instruction is to *read each question* and make sure you know what is wanted. The second most important instruction is to *time yourself properly* so that you answer every question. The third most important instruction is to *answer every question*. Guess if you have to but include something for each question. Remember that you will receive no credit for a blank and will probably receive some credit if you write something in answer to an essay question. If you guess a letter – say "B" for a multiple-choice question – you may have guessed right. If you leave a blank as an answer to a multiple-choice question, the examiners may respect your feelings but it will not add a point to your score. Some exams may penalize you for wrong answers, so in such cases *only*, you may not want to guess unless you have some basis for your answer.

7) Suggestions
    a. Objective-type questions
        1. Examine the question booklet for proper sequence of pages and questions
        2. Read all instructions carefully
        3. Skip any question which seems too difficult; return to it after all other questions have been answered
        4. Apportion your time properly; do not spend too much time on any single question or group of questions

5. Note and underline key words – *all, most, fewest, least, best, worst, same, opposite*, etc.
6. Pay particular attention to negatives
7. Note unusual option, e.g., unduly long, short, complex, different or similar in content to the body of the question
8. Observe the use of "hedging" words – *probably, may, most likely*, etc.
9. Make sure that your answer is put next to the same number as the question
10. Do not second-guess unless you have good reason to believe the second answer is definitely more correct
11. Cross out original answer if you decide another answer is more accurate; do not erase until you are ready to hand your paper in
12. Answer all questions; guess unless instructed otherwise
13. Leave time for review

   b. Essay questions
   1. Read each question carefully
   2. Determine exactly what is wanted. Underline key words or phrases.
   3. Decide on outline or paragraph answer
   4. Include many different points and elements unless asked to develop any one or two points or elements
   5. Show impartiality by giving pros and cons unless directed to select one side only
   6. Make and write down any assumptions you find necessary to answer the questions
   7. Watch your English, grammar, punctuation and choice of words
   8. Time your answers; don't crowd material

8) Answering the essay question

Most essay questions can be answered by framing the specific response around several key words or ideas. Here are a few such key words or ideas:

M's: manpower, materials, methods, money, management
P's: purpose, program, policy, plan, procedure, practice, problems, pitfalls, personnel, public relations

   a. Six basic steps in handling problems:
   1. Preliminary plan and background development
   2. Collect information, data and facts
   3. Analyze and interpret information, data and facts
   4. Analyze and develop solutions as well as make recommendations
   5. Prepare report and sell recommendations
   6. Install recommendations and follow up effectiveness

   b. Pitfalls to avoid
   1. *Taking things for granted* – A statement of the situation does not necessarily imply that each of the elements is necessarily true; for example, a complaint may be invalid and biased so that all that can be taken for granted is that a complaint has been registered

2. *Considering only one side of a situation* – Wherever possible, indicate several alternatives and then point out the reasons you selected the best one
3. *Failing to indicate follow up* – Whenever your answer indicates action on your part, make certain that you will take proper follow-up action to see how successful your recommendations, procedures or actions turn out to be
4. *Taking too long in answering any single question* – Remember to time your answers properly

## IX. AFTER THE TEST

Scoring procedures differ in detail among civil service jurisdictions although the general principles are the same. Whether the papers are hand-scored or graded by machine we have described, they are nearly always graded by number. That is, the person who marks the paper knows only the number – never the name – of the applicant. Not until all the papers have been graded will they be matched with names. If other tests, such as training and experience or oral interview ratings have been given, scores will be combined. Different parts of the examination usually have different weights. For example, the written test might count 60 percent of the final grade, and a rating of training and experience 40 percent. In many jurisdictions, veterans will have a certain number of points added to their grades.

After the final grade has been determined, the names are placed in grade order and an eligible list is established. There are various methods for resolving ties between those who get the same final grade – probably the most common is to place first the name of the person whose application was received first. Job offers are made from the eligible list in the order the names appear on it. You will be notified of your grade and your rank as soon as all these computations have been made. This will be done as rapidly as possible.

People who are found to meet the requirements in the announcement are called "eligibles." Their names are put on a list of eligible candidates. An eligible's chances of getting a job depend on how high he stands on this list and how fast agencies are filling jobs from the list.

When a job is to be filled from a list of eligibles, the agency asks for the names of people on the list of eligibles for that job. When the civil service commission receives this request, it sends to the agency the names of the three people highest on this list. Or, if the job to be filled has specialized requirements, the office sends the agency the names of the top three persons who meet these requirements from the general list.

The appointing officer makes a choice from among the three people whose names were sent to him. If the selected person accepts the appointment, the names of the others are put back on the list to be considered for future openings.

That is the rule in hiring from all kinds of eligible lists, whether they are for typist, carpenter, chemist, or something else. For every vacancy, the appointing officer has his choice of any one of the top three eligibles on the list. This explains why the person whose name is on top of the list sometimes does not get an appointment when some of the persons lower on the list do. If the appointing officer chooses the second or third eligible, the No. 1 eligible does not get a job at once, but stays on the list until he is appointed or the list is terminated.

# X. HOW TO PASS THE INTERVIEW TEST

The examination for which you applied requires an oral interview test. You have already taken the written test and you are now being called for the interview test – the final part of the formal examination.

You may think that it is not possible to prepare for an interview test and that there are no procedures to follow during an interview. Our purpose is to point out some things you can do in advance that will help you and some good rules to follow and pitfalls to avoid while you are being interviewed.

*What is an interview supposed to test?*

The written examination is designed to test the technical knowledge and competence of the candidate; the oral is designed to evaluate intangible qualities, not readily measured otherwise, and to establish a list showing the relative fitness of each candidate – as measured against his competitors – for the position sought. Scoring is not on the basis of "right" and "wrong," but on a sliding scale of values ranging from "not passable" to "outstanding." As a matter of fact, it is possible to achieve a relatively low score without a single "incorrect" answer because of evident weakness in the qualities being measured.

Occasionally, an examination may consist entirely of an oral test – either an individual or a group oral. In such cases, information is sought concerning the technical knowledges and abilities of the candidate, since there has been no written examination for this purpose. More commonly, however, an oral test is used to supplement a written examination.

*Who conducts interviews?*

The composition of oral boards varies among different jurisdictions. In nearly all, a representative of the personnel department serves as chairman. One of the members of the board may be a representative of the department in which the candidate would work. In some cases, "outside experts" are used, and, frequently, a businessman or some other representative of the general public is asked to serve. Labor and management or other special groups may be represented. The aim is to secure the services of experts in the appropriate field.

However the board is composed, it is a good idea (and not at all improper or unethical) to ascertain in advance of the interview who the members are and what groups they represent. When you are introduced to them, you will have some idea of their backgrounds and interests, and at least you will not stutter and stammer over their names.

*What should be done before the interview?*

While knowledge about the board members is useful and takes some of the surprise element out of the interview, there is other preparation which is more substantive. It *is* possible to prepare for an oral interview – in several ways:

**1) Keep a copy of your application and review it carefully before the interview**

This may be the only document before the oral board, and the starting point of the interview. Know what education and experience you have listed there, and the sequence and dates of all of it. Sometimes the board will ask you to review the highlights of your experience for them; you should not have to hem and haw doing it.

**2) Study the class specification and the examination announcement**

Usually, the oral board has one or both of these to guide them. The qualities, characteristics or knowledges required by the position sought are stated in these documents. They offer valuable clues as to the nature of the oral interview. For example, if the job involves supervisory responsibilities, the announcement will usually indicate that knowledge of modern supervisory methods and the qualifications of the candidate as a supervisor will be tested. If so, you can expect such questions, frequently in the form of a hypothetical situation which you are expected to solve. NEVER go into an oral without knowledge of the duties and responsibilities of the job you seek.

### 3) Think through each qualification required

Try to visualize the kind of questions you would ask if you were a board member. How well could you answer them? Try especially to appraise your own knowledge and background in each area, *measured against the job sought*, and identify any areas in which you are weak. Be critical and realistic – do not flatter yourself.

### 4) Do some general reading in areas in which you feel you may be weak

For example, if the job involves supervision and your past experience has NOT, some general reading in supervisory methods and practices, particularly in the field of human relations, might be useful. Do NOT study agency procedures or detailed manuals. The oral board will be testing your understanding and capacity, not your memory.

### 5) Get a good night's sleep and watch your general health and mental attitude

You will want a clear head at the interview. Take care of a cold or any other minor ailment, and of course, no hangovers.

*What should be done on the day of the interview?*

Now comes the day of the interview itself. Give yourself plenty of time to get there. Plan to arrive somewhat ahead of the scheduled time, particularly if your appointment is in the fore part of the day. If a previous candidate fails to appear, the board might be ready for you a bit early. By early afternoon an oral board is almost invariably behind schedule if there are many candidates, and you may have to wait. Take along a book or magazine to read, or your application to review, but leave any extraneous material in the waiting room when you go in for your interview. In any event, relax and compose yourself.

The matter of dress is important. The board is forming impressions about you – from your experience, your manners, your attitude, and your appearance. Give your personal appearance careful attention. Dress your best, but not your flashiest. Choose conservative, appropriate clothing, and be sure it is immaculate. This is a business interview, and your appearance should indicate that you regard it as such. Besides, being well groomed and properly dressed will help boost your confidence.

Sooner or later, someone will call your name and escort you into the interview room. *This is it*. From here on you are on your own. It is too late for any more preparation. But remember, you asked for this opportunity to prove your fitness, and you are here because your request was granted.

*What happens when you go in?*

The usual sequence of events will be as follows: The clerk (who is often the board stenographer) will introduce you to the chairman of the oral board, who will introduce you to the other members of the board. Acknowledge the introductions before you sit down. Do not be surprised if you find a microphone facing you or a stenotypist sitting by. Oral interviews are usually recorded in the event of an appeal or other review.

Usually the chairman of the board will open the interview by reviewing the highlights of your education and work experience from your application – primarily for the benefit of the other members of the board, as well as to get the material into the record. Do not interrupt or comment unless there is an error or significant misinterpretation; if that is the case, do not hesitate. But do not quibble about insignificant matters. Also, he will usually ask you some question about your education, experience or your present job – partly to get you to start talking and to establish the interviewing "rapport." He may start the actual questioning, or turn it over to one of the other members. Frequently, each member undertakes the questioning on a particular area, one in which he is perhaps most competent, so you can expect each member to participate in the examination. Because time is limited, you may also expect some rather abrupt switches in the direction the questioning takes, so do not be upset by it. Normally, a board member will not pursue a single line of questioning unless he discovers a particular strength or weakness.

After each member has participated, the chairman will usually ask whether any member has any further questions, then will ask you if you have anything you wish to add. Unless you are expecting this question, it may floor you. Worse, it may start you off on an extended, extemporaneous speech. The board is not usually seeking more information. The question is principally to offer you a last opportunity to present further qualifications or to indicate that you have nothing to add. So, if you feel that a significant qualification or characteristic has been overlooked, it is proper to point it out in a sentence or so. Do not compliment the board on the thoroughness of their examination – they have been sketchy, and you know it. If you wish, merely say, "No thank you, I have nothing further to add." This is a point where you can "talk yourself out" of a good impression or fail to present an important bit of information. Remember, *you close the interview yourself.*

The chairman will then say, "That is all, Mr. _____, thank you." Do not be startled; the interview is over, and quicker than you think. Thank him, gather your belongings and take your leave. Save your sigh of relief for the other side of the door.


*How to put your best foot forward*
Throughout this entire process, you may feel that the board individually and collectively is trying to pierce your defenses, seek out your hidden weaknesses and embarrass and confuse you. Actually, this is not true. They are obliged to make an appraisal of your qualifications for the job you are seeking, and they want to see you in your best light. Remember, they must interview all candidates and a non-cooperative candidate may become a failure in spite of their best efforts to bring out his qualifications. Here are 15 suggestions that will help you:

**1) Be natural – Keep your attitude confident, not cocky**
If you are not confident that you can do the job, do not expect the board to be. Do not apologize for your weaknesses, try to bring out your strong points. The board is interested in a positive, not negative, presentation. Cockiness will antagonize any board member and make him wonder if you are covering up a weakness by a false show of strength.

**2) Get comfortable, but don't lounge or sprawl**
Sit erectly but not stiffly. A careless posture may lead the board to conclude that you are careless in other things, or at least that you are not impressed by the importance of the occasion. Either conclusion is natural, even if incorrect. Do not fuss with your clothing, a pencil or an ashtray. Your hands may occasionally be useful to emphasize a point; do not let them become a point of distraction.

**3) Do not wisecrack or make small talk**
This is a serious situation, and your attitude should show that you consider it as such. Further, the time of the board is limited – they do not want to waste it, and neither should you.

### 4) Do not exaggerate your experience or abilities

In the first place, from information in the application or other interviews and sources, the board may know more about you than you think. Secondly, you probably will not get away with it. An experienced board is rather adept at spotting such a situation, so do not take the chance.

### 5) If you know a board member, do not make a point of it, yet do not hide it

Certainly you are not fooling him, and probably not the other members of the board. Do not try to take advantage of your acquaintanceship – it will probably do you little good.

### 6) Do not dominate the interview

Let the board do that. They will give you the clues – do not assume that you have to do all the talking. Realize that the board has a number of questions to ask you, and do not try to take up all the interview time by showing off your extensive knowledge of the answer to the first one.

### 7) Be attentive

You only have 20 minutes or so, and you should keep your attention at its sharpest throughout. When a member is addressing a problem or question to you, give him your undivided attention. Address your reply principally to him, but do not exclude the other board members.

### 8) Do not interrupt

A board member may be stating a problem for you to analyze. He will ask you a question when the time comes. Let him state the problem, and wait for the question.

### 9) Make sure you understand the question

Do not try to answer until you are sure what the question is. If it is not clear, restate it in your own words or ask the board member to clarify it for you. However, do not haggle about minor elements.

### 10) Reply promptly but not hastily

A common entry on oral board rating sheets is "candidate responded readily," or "candidate hesitated in replies." Respond as promptly and quickly as you can, but do not jump to a hasty, ill-considered answer.

### 11) Do not be peremptory in your answers

A brief answer is proper – but do not fire your answer back. That is a losing game from your point of view. The board member can probably ask questions much faster than you can answer them.

### 12) Do not try to create the answer you think the board member wants

He is interested in what kind of mind you have and how it works – not in playing games. Furthermore, he can usually spot this practice and will actually grade you down on it.

### 13) Do not switch sides in your reply merely to agree with a board member

Frequently, a member will take a contrary position merely to draw you out and to see if you are willing and able to defend your point of view. Do not start a debate, yet do not surrender a good position. If a position is worth taking, it is worth defending.

**14) Do not be afraid to admit an error in judgment if you are shown to be wrong**

The board knows that you are forced to reply without any opportunity for careful consideration. Your answer may be demonstrably wrong. If so, admit it and get on with the interview.

**15) Do not dwell at length on your present job**

The opening question may relate to your present assignment. Answer the question but do not go into an extended discussion. You are being examined for a *new* job, not your present one. As a matter of fact, try to phrase ALL your answers in terms of the job for which you are being examined.

*Basis of Rating*

Probably you will forget most of these "do's" and "don'ts" when you walk into the oral interview room. Even remembering them all will not ensure you a passing grade. Perhaps you did not have the qualifications in the first place. But remembering them will help you to put your best foot forward, without treading on the toes of the board members.

Rumor and popular opinion to the contrary notwithstanding, an oral board wants you to make the best appearance possible. They know you are under pressure – but they also want to see how you respond to it as a guide to what your reaction would be under the pressures of the job you seek. They will be influenced by the degree of poise you display, the personal traits you show and the manner in which you respond.


ABOUT THIS BOOK

This book contains tests divided into Examination Sections. Go through each test, answering every question in the margin. We have also attached a sample answer sheet at the back of the book that can be removed and used. At the end of each test look at the answer key and check your answers. On the ones you got wrong, look at the right answer choice and learn. Do not fill in the answers first. Do not memorize the questions and answers, but understand the answer and principles involved. On your test, the questions will likely be different from the samples. Questions are changed and new ones added. If you understand these past questions you should have success with any changes that arise. Tests may consist of several types of questions. We have additional books on each subject should more study be advisable or necessary for you. Finally, the more you study, the better prepared you will be. This book is intended to be the last thing you study before you walk into the examination room. Prior study of relevant texts is also recommended. NLC publishes some of these in our Fundamental Series. Knowledge and good sense are important factors in passing your exam. Good luck also helps. So now study this Passbook, absorb the material contained within and take that knowledge into the examination. Then do your best to pass that exam.

# EXAMINATION SECTION

# EXAMINATION SECTION
## TEST 1

DIRECTIONS: Each question or incomplete statement is followed by several suggested answers or completions. Select the one that BEST answers the question or completes the statement. *PRINT THE LETTER OF THE CORRECT ANSWER IN THE SPACE AT THE RIGHT.*

1. The philosophy of case work is based upon the

    A. recognition of the dignity of the human person
    B. place of the agency in the community
    C. importance of planning realistically with clients
    D. role of the worker in case work treatment

2. Social case work aims CHIEFLY to

    A. give material assistance and help the client achieve success
    B. find the reasons for the person's difficulty and refer him for help to the proper source
    C. help the person through a professional relationship to gain a better understanding of his problem and to help him make a satisfactory adjustment
    D. improve the person's environment

3. The interview in case work is used CHIEFLY

    A. to get proof of data required in evaluating the client's problems and resources
    B. as a tool to explore with the client his feelings about his problem, as well as about the problem itself, so as to arrive at a plan of treatment
    C. because it is less expensive than other methods of work
    D. for statistical purposes on the basis of the worker's record

4. The case work relationship between the worker and the client is important CHIEFLY because it

    A. is a friendly relationship which the client needs at times
    B. provides an opportunity for the client to talk things out
    C. is a professional relationship to which the worker brings specific knowledge and skills to help another person
    D. provides concentrated attention to problems over a short period of time

5. The case worker, to be MOST effective in helping another person, must

    A. be free from prejudice of any kind
    B. have a wide knowledge of the individual's cultural background
    C. have received help himself in order to better understand the client's feelings
    D. be aware as much as possible about his own feelings regarding his client

6. One of the BEST known marks of the mature person is the ability to

    A. control his feelings in difficult situations
    B. defer future pleasures or gratifications for long-term goals
    C. take things as they come, trusting in luck
    D. enjoy a great many outside interests in life

7. An adult with a mental age of 9 years was regarded psychologically as

   A. of normal mentality
   B. a moron
   C. an imbecile
   D. an idiot

8. The one of the following conditions which bears NO causative relationship to mental deficiency is

   A. heredity
   B. cerebral defect
   C. early postnatal trauma
   D. dementia

9. Physical conditions which are caused by emotional conflicts are GENERALLY referred to as being

   A. psycho-social
   B. hypochondriacal
   C. psychosomatic
   D. psychotic

10. Of the following conditions, the one in which anxiety is NOT generally found is

    A. psychopathic personality
    B. mild hysteria
    C. psychoneurosis
    D. compulsive-obsessive personality

11. Kleptomania may BEST be described as a

    A. neurotic drive to accumulate personal property through compulsive acts in order to dispose of it to others with whom one wishes friendship
    B. type of neurosis which manifests itself in an uncontrollable impulse to steal without economic motivation
    C. psychopathic trait which is probably hereditary in nature
    D. manifestation of punishment-inviting behavior based upon guilt feelings for some other crime or wrongdoing, fantasied or real, committed as a child

12. The one of the following tests which is NOT ordinarily used as a projective technique is the

    A. Wechsler Bellevue Scale
    B. Rorschach Test
    C. Thematic Apperception Test
    D. Jung Free Association Test

13. An outstanding personality test in use at the present time is the Rorschach Test. Of the following considerations, the GREATEST value of this test to the psychiatrist and social worker is that it

    A. provides practical recommendations with reference to further educational and vocational training possibilities for the person tested
    B. reveals in quick, concise form the hereditary factors affecting the individual personality
    C. helps in substantiating a diagnosis of juvenile delinquency
    D. helps in a diagnostic formulation and in determining differential treatment

14. Of the following, the one through which ethical values are MOST generally acquired is     14._____

    A. heredity
    B. early training in school
    C. admonition and strict corrective measures by parents and other supervising adults
    D. integration into the self of parental values and attitudes

15. Records show that MOST crimes in the United States are committed by persons _____ years of age.     15._____

    A. under 18           B. from 18 to 25
    C. from 30 to 40      D. above 40

16. According to current theories of criminology, the one of the following which is regarded as the MOST important cause of delinquency is     16._____

    A. personality maladjustment
    B. lack of proper housing
    C. mental deficiency
    D. community indifference to the need for recreational facilities

17. Delinquent behavior is MOST generally a result of     17._____

    A. living and growing up in an environment that is both socially and financially deprived
    B. a lack of educational opportunity for development of individual skills
    C. multiple factors - psychological, bio-social, emotional, and environmental
    D. low frustration tolerance of many parents toward problems of married life

18. Unmarried mothers USUALLY     18._____

    A. come from homes of poor economic status
    B. have had poor moral training in their youth
    C. are amoral or have little or no feeling of guilt
    D. all of the above

19. Alcoholism in the United States is USUALLY caused by     19._____

    A. the sense of frustration in one's work
    B. inadequacy of recreational facilities
    C. neurotic conflicts expressed in drinking excessively
    D. shyness and timidity

20. The MOST distinctive characteristic of the chronic alcoholic is that he drinks alcohol     20._____

    A. socially           B. compulsively
    C. periodically       D. secretly

21. *The chronic alcoholic is the person who cannot face reality without alcohol, and yet whose adequate adjustment to reality is impossible so long as he uses alcohol.*     21._____
    On the basis of this quotation, it is MOST reasonable to conclude that individuals over-indulge in alcohol because alcohol

A. deadens the sense of conflict, giving the individual an illusion of social competence and a feeling of well-being and success
B. provides the individual with an outlet to display his feelings of good-fellowship and cheerfulness which are characteristic of his extroverted personality
C. affords an escape technique from habitual irrational fears, but does not affect rational fears
D. offers an escape from imagery and feelings of superiority which cause tension and anxiety

22. The one of the following drugs to which a person is LEAST likely to become addicted is

A. opium  B. morphine  C. marijuana  D. heroin

23. Teenagers who become addicted to the use of drugs are MOST generally

A. mentally defective
B. paranoid
C. normally adventurous
D. emotionally disturbed

24. In the light of the current high rate of addiction to drugs among youths throughout the country, the one of the following statements which is generally considered to be LEAST correct is that

A. a relatively large number of children and youths who experiment with drugs become addicts
B. youths who use narcotics do so because of some emotional and personality disturbance
C. youthful addicts are found largely among those who suffer to an abnormal extent deprivations in their personal development and growth
D. the great majority of youthful addicts have had unfortunate home experiences and practically no contact with established community agencies

25. The Social Service Exchange is utilized by probation officers PRIMARILY in order to

A. facilitate the operation of the Interstate Compact for the transfer of probationers
B. secure a complete criminal record of the defendant awaiting sentence
C. secure a listing of agencies which have known the defendant or his family
D. acquire a developmental history of the defendant

Questions 26-32.

DIRECTIONS: Column I lists terms and Column II gives definitions. For each term listed in Column I, select its definition from Column II, and write the letter which precedes this definition.

COLUMN I

26. acquittal
27. arrest
28. citation
29. commitment
30. indictment
31. recidivism
32. rendition

COLUMN II

A. surrender by one state of a person found in that state for prosecution in another state having jurisdiction to try the charge

B. an official summons or notice to a person to appear before a court

C. the act of taking a person into custody by authority of law

D. a formal written statement charging one or more persons with an offense as formulated by the prosecutor and found by a grand jury

E. bringing the accused before a court to answer a minimal charge

F. an accusation of any offense or unlawful state of affairs originating with a grand jury from their own knowledge or observation

G. consignment to a place of official confinement of a person found guilty of a crime

H. finding the accused not guilty of a crime after trial

I. agreement to appear in court upon request, without bond

J. reversion or relapse into prior criminal habits even after punishment

26._____
27._____
28._____
29._____
30._____
31._____
32._____

33. According to the statutes, a misdemeanor is an offense  33.___

    A. which is punishable by not more than an indeterminate term of from two to four years in a state prison
    B. not accompanied by physical violence
    C. for which reformatory sentence is mandatory unless sentence is suspended
    D. punishable by not more than one year of imprisonment

34. A person who is found guilty of a misdemeanor in a court may be kept under probationary supervision for  34.___

    A. a maximum of one year
    B. a period not to exceed one-half of the prison term prescribed by law
    C. a maximum of three years
    D. as long as the court desires

35. According to the State Griminal Procedure Law, the period of probation in the case of a child may NOT extend beyond  35.___

    A. his minority
    B. three years from the date of disposition
    C. the maximum time for which he might have been institutionalized
    D. the time required for him to make an adequate adjustment

36. According to the Criminal Procedure Law, the court which imposed the conditions of probation may  36.___

    A. not change them under any circumstances
    B. subsequently modify these conditions
    C. revise them only after one year of probation
    D. revise but not increase them

37. In cases of adult offenders, probation differs from parole in that probation involves  37.___

    A. suspension of sentence
    B. supervision after imprisonment
    C. supervision as a preliminary to parole
    D. un unlimited period of surveillance

38. One of the duties of the probation officer during pre-sentence investigations and the supervision process is the consideration of evidence.  38.___
    Of the following statements relating to the different types of evidence, the one which is LEAST accurate is that

    A. real evidence consists of any facts which are secured by first-hand experience
    B. testimonial evidence is the assertion of a human being
    C. hearsay evidence has little or no validity in probation practice
    D. expert evidence is the testimony of a person with specialized knowledge of or skill in a particular field

39. *The effect of rumors may be temporary or lasting. If they are reinforced and if there is no appreciable conflict with other and then with newer impulses, they are likely to persist. The rumor-engendered impression, moreover, is often the first reaction to an event. Subsequent information labors under a psychological handicap even when it is perceived. If a man is ruined by lies which people have the desire to believe, only compelling truths can resurrect him. The truths, though, will not be responded to eagerly, and they most probably will not drive out all the effects from the past.*
    Of the following, the statement which is MOST accurate on the basis of the above paragraph is that

    A. rumor-engendered impressions are readily obliterated if disproved by compelling truths
    B. uninformed rumors should not be spread since they usually ruin people's lives
    C. false rumors are disproved with difficulty, and the first impression of uncontested and disproved false rumors is likely to continue
    D. unlike the normal reaction to the rumor proved false, there is a psychological handicap in accepting the uncontested rumor

40. Of the following, the MAIN reason for keeping a case record in probation or parole supervision is to

    A. present a verified picture of all legal aspects of the case
    B. provide a complete and objective understanding of the person through knowledge gained from relatives, friends, and other agencies
    C. improve the quality of service to the probationer and to help the probation officer to understand him and his situation
    D. give a realistic picture of the employment and recreational activities of the person in order to evaluate his progress toward rehabilitation

---

## KEY (CORRECT ANSWERS)

| | | | |
|---|---|---|---|
| 1. A | 11. B | 21. A | 31. J |
| 2. C | 12. A | 22. C | 32. A |
| 3. B | 13. D | 23. D | 33. D |
| 4. C | 14. D | 24. A | 34. C |
| 5. D | 15. B | 25. C | 35. A |
| 6. A | 16. A | 26. H | 36. B |
| 7. B | 17. C | 27. C | 37. A |
| 8. D | 18. D | 28. B | 38. C |
| 9. C | 19. C | 29. G | 39. C |
| 10. A | 20. B | 30. D | 40. C |

# TEST 2

DIRECTIONS: Each question or incomplete statement is followed by several suggested answers or completions. Select the one that BEST answers the question or completes the statement. *PRINT THE LETTER OF THE CORRECT ANSWER IN THE SPACE AT THE RIGHT.*

1. The MOST accurate of the following statements concerning probation case records is that they

    A. are generically different from those in use in the private case work field
    B. differ radically from the procedural records of the court
    C. should of necessity place less emphasis on the treatment than on the investigation of a person on probation
    D. should emphasize surveillance factors of probation

2. Of the following reasons for maintaining records in the probation department, the one which has the LEAST significance to the agency and the probation officer is that

    A. case recording is an essential adjunct to the practice of case work
    B. accurate and current case records facilitate treatment
    C. case records represent the agency's knowledge, insight, experience, efforts, and plans in individual situations
    D. case records represent evidence with which to deny false accusations and derogatory evaluative statements arising in the community

3. The method of case recording which reflects the interaction between the client and the social worker around the problem as the client sees it and feels about it is known as

    A. chronological         B. process
    C. summary               D. topical

4. The one of the following which is the MOST important asset for a probation officer is

    A. a well-integrated personality
    B. expert knowledge of crime causation
    C. comprehensive knowledge of community resources
    D. good health to enable the office to cope with the hazards of probation work

5. A probation officer, newly assigned as a worker in a legalistic agency structure, must set goals for himself as a learner in a new experience.
The one of the following which MOST comprehensively and clearly states the learning goals of the new probation officer is to gain

    A. a comprehensive knowledge of the basic structure of the agency and the laws under which it operates
    B. a clear understanding of the objectives of the programs of the agency and of the underlying philosophy which governs the manner in which these programs are administered
    C. the integration of knowledge, development of skills in practice and growth in personal emotional structure necessary to enable him to help others most effectively
    D. the ability to recognize distress and signs of emotional disturbance in people and to treat symptomatic behavior while working within the agency framework

6. The one of the following statements which is LEAST accurate is:

   A. The type of evidence available in making a diagnosis of a person under investigation by a probation officer generally is not of a probative value equal to that of facts found in the exact sciences
   B. The rehabilitative treatment of a probationer lacks the precision used in treating physical diseases
   C. The vast background of experience in probation work today makes it possible for the probation officer to diagnose with certainty the personality and character of the probationer
   D. In considering evidence during an investigation, the probation officer can never be sure whether some fact has been overlooked that might alter the entire analysis

   6.\_\_\_\_

7. The MOST accurate of the following statements with respect to reciprocal state legislation to compel the support of dependent wives and children, better known as the Uniform Support of Dependents Law, is:

   A. The amount of support allotted to women and children has been made uniform throughout the United States
   B. Provision has been made for the deserted wife to make the complaint in the state of residence and for the order of support against her husband to be made in the state where her husband now resides
   C. Sufficient federal funds have been provided to make it possible for the deserted wife to travel to the state where the deserting husband has been located and there make the proper complaint for support
   D. The legal requirements of extradition concerning deserting husbands have been eased, thereby facilitating their return to the state where the spouse resides to face appropriate criminal action

   7.\_\_\_\_

8. The one of the following statements which contains the basic principle upon which *Aggressive Case Work* GENERALLY operates is:

   A. When a client applies for help with a delinquent child, the worker, following a complete study of the problem, forcefully and very definitely defines the solution of the problem to the client
   B. The social worker waits until the neglect of a child by his parents reaches a point where the court should take action and then proceeds to remove the child from his home
   C. New social work techniques are used to arouse the client's interest so that he voluntarily requests aid
   D. The social worker goes out to meet the client in his own setting

   8.\_\_\_\_

9. Treatment of the delinquent child must be based on the child's individual needs PRIMARILY because

   A. the child's needs are usually for adequate recreational facilities and better home conditions
   B. social treatment depends upon social diagnosis, and sound diagnosis requires knowledge of the person
   C. behavior is usually determined by environment, which is unique for each person
   D. the child's needs are usually less complicated than those of an adult

   9.\_\_\_\_

10. It has been said that the probation officer working with a delinquent child *becomes for the child the symbol of the authority against which he rebels.* The task of the probation officer is to convert what appears to be a handicap into an asset.
Of the following approaches to this problem, the one which serves the probation officer MOST advantageously is to

    A. disguise his role of authority by becoming a friend to the child, who will then respond in a more personal way by talking freely about himself and his experiences
    B. strengthen the parents so that they will relax their parental authoritative role and be more permissive in their discipline of the child
    C. maintain his authority while offering guidance and counsel on the basis of disciplined concern for the child, genuine warmth, and willingness and capacity to enter into his feelings and thinking about persons, situations, and things
    D. refer the case to an agency in the community where the non-authoritative setting will permit reaching the child on a social and psychological basis through the use of treatment techniques for emotionally disturbed children

11. Of the following statements relating to probation of known alcoholics, the one which is MOST accurate is:

    A. In order to help an alcoholic person under supervision, a probation officer should consider it important for the family to understand something of the probationer's problem
    B. Referral of alcoholic probationers to medical facilities for the administration of certain drugs has proven successful in practically all cases
    C. Research to date demonstrates that, in general, alcoholics on probation make an easy and adequate adjustment
    D. Most domestic relations problems are caused by alcoholics or heavy drinkers

12. Probation officers frequently encounter problems of young adults, either single or married, with deep, unresolved dependency conflicts who cannot make mature adjustments in their work, living arrangements, or handling of their marital and parent-child relationships. The one of the following which is MOST appropriate in case work with individuals or families presenting problems of this type is

    A. environment service, affording immediate adjustments of an external character
    B. specific advice and concrete suggestions given directly by the case worker upon his own initiative
    C. case work treatment through which the person learns to handle his situation realistically with lessened anxiety as a result of a clearer understanding of deep-seated, repressed emotional material
    D. supportive counseling in helping the person to gain some beginning insight into his basic problem so that he can be helped, if need is indicated, to move on to psychiatric treatment

13. In supervising an unemployed probationer, the one of the following actions which ordinarily represents GOOD probation practice is to

    A. refer the probationer immediately to the State Unemployment Bureau
    B. encourage the probationer and give him supportive help in using his own initiative to secure employment

C. refer the probationer to personal employer contacts known to the probation officer
D. fix a time limit for the probationer to get a job before returning him to court for violation of probation

14. The majority of cases coming to a court because of marital discord are presented at a time of crisis.
Of the following approaches, the one which is MOST essential to the probation officer in offering help to a family in this situation is

    A. early analysis of his own attitudes and reactions in differentiating between factors already present in the personalities of the husband and wife and of situational factors
    B. immediate determination of the legal aspects of the marriage problem and recognition and handling of transference and counter-transference in the case work relationship
    C. establishing of a relationship which will enable the client to express his feelings and to present the problem as he sees it, thus enabling the probation officer to arrive at a sound diagnostic judgment
    D. offering of a relationship at a level that will provide a vent to the husband and wife, endeavoring to use psychological support to direct them towards reconciliation

15. Mr. X, while on probation on a charge of desertion, again absconds, leaving his family without provision for support. The one of the following actions to be taken FIRST by the probation officer in apprehending the probationer is to

    A. file a probation warrant with the local police department
    B. prepare a violation of probation report requesting the court to issue a bench warrant
    C. request the court to revoke the man's probation and advise his wife to immediately make a new complaint of desertion
    D. interview the deserted wife in order to understand her feelings about her husband's desertion and to discuss with her, if she wishes, the possible whereabouts of the probationer

16. A boy of 15, on probation for one year in the Children's Court on an original petition of delinquency made by his inadequate mother, has shown no improvement in his behavior, is beyond her control, and is associating with a gang consisting of other seriously delinquent boys.
Of the following courses of action, the one which is MOST advisable for the probation officer to pursue is to

    A. refer the boy for psychiatric evaluation or recommendation to determine whether he should be committed to an institution where he might receive treatment in a controlled environment
    B. refer the family to a social agency for counseling to improve the home situation
    C. arrange to have more frequent interviews with the mother
    D. caution the boy that unless he improves his behavior and disassociates himself from the gang, the probation officer will be forced to recommend commitment to an institution

17. An adolescent girl held as a material witness in a case of rape expresses strong hostility towards her mother, whom she claims always favored her younger brother. The mother says, in an interview, that she was always devoted to her own mother, now deceased, but that she was never able to confide in her or feel that she was understood by her. This knowledge of the mother's earlier experiences may provide a clue to the probation officer in understanding causative factors in the girl's behavior.
Of the following explanations, the one which MOST likely accounts for the poor relationship between mother and daughter is that the

      17.____

    A. mother's greater interest in and warmth for her son would indicate that she had a better relationship with her own father than with her mother
    B. mother of the girl had lacked a warm, trusting relationship with her own mother and, therefore, provided an overpermissive atmosphere in her home for her daughter, believing that this would create a closer relationship between them
    C. girl's behavior springs from a fantasied maturity which is a spurious and unreal assumption of an adult status, often a temporary phase in adolescent growth
    D. mother of the girl probably had not worked through problems in relationship with her own mother and was unable, therefore, to establish a sound relationship with her daughter

18. A girl of 19, adjudicated as a wayward minor and placed on probation, is discovered by the probation officer to be a prostitute, although this has not yet come to the attention of the authorities.
The one of the following courses of action which is MOST advisable for the probation officer to pursue in these circumstances is to

      18.____

    A. recommend that probation be revoked and that the girl be committed to an institution
    B. advise the girl that unless she discontinues this behavior the probation officer will have to report it to the court
    C. give the girl an opportunity to work out the problem for herself
    D. re-evaluate the case, discussing the matter with the probation officer's supervisor and determining appropriate action to take for the best interests of the community and the probationer

19. Mrs. A comes to a social agency asking for help with her 8-year-old son who is a truant from school and is generally willful and disobedient. Mr. A travels a good deal and is seldom at home. He has had very little part in the rearing of the child.
Of the following actions, the one which the case worker should take FIRST is to

      19.____

    A. see the child in order to learn from him why he is misbehaving
    B. arrange to see the father in order to advise him to change his job
    C. explore with Mr. A her feelings about the child as well as her feelings about her husband's part in the family picture
    D. visit the school to discover the cause of the difficulty there

20. A 17-year-old male on probation in the Family Court tells his probation officer that he resents reporting to him because he was innocent of the crime for which he was placed on probation. In addition, he states he dislikes the probation officer.
In this situation, the one of the following courses of action which the probation officer should pursue is to

      20.____

A. encourage the probationer to seek legal assistance to reopen the case
B. adopt a firm attitude indicating that he is not interested in the probationer's guilt or innocence and insisting that he comply with the probation conditions
C. seek to understand the reasons why the probationer dislikes him, at the same time indicating to him that he is free to explore legal assistance regarding his original offense
D. consider the probationer as rebellious and a potential community threat, recommending that probation be revoked

21. *A person's behavior is both shaped and judged by the expectations he and his culture have invested in his status and the major social roles he carries.*
 According to this principle, a caseworker can BEST make effective professional judgments and plan proper treatment if he recognizes that

   A. the client's problem may stem from role conflicts
   B. the client faces difficulties serenely once he knows what society expects of him
   C. cultural values have little to do with a client's status
   D. the status-seeking individual is not able to comprehend the function of cultural values in his life

21._____

22. The diagnostic approach in social casework, often called the Freudian School, has as its basic premise the

   A. investigation of past events of the client's life experiences and functioning in order to understand his present situation
   B. study of the subconscious mind of the client as to his present attitude and understanding about his situation
   C. examination of behavioral motivation of the client
   D. solution of the client's problem through aptitude testing and group therapy

22._____

23. There is implicit in casework an acceptance of a client's value system which may be different from that of the caseworker.
 Of the following, the MOST valid conclusion to be derived from this statement is that

   A. clients do not have moral standards
   B. the caseworkers' standards are always stricter than the clients' standards
   C. cultural patterns have little effect on value systems by either clients or caseworkers
   D. a caseworker has no right to insist on conformity of a client's behavior with his own standards

23._____

24. The establishment and maintenance of a professional relationship with a client is stressed in casework. This relationship should be

   A. clear, business-like, and delimited by the agency function
   B. permissive, friendly, and kindly, with the pace determined by the client
   C. warm, enabling, and consciously controlled by the caseworker
   D. variable and unpredictable because of the fluctuations in client need

24._____

25. There is great interest being shown currently in the possible merger of the child welfare and family casework fields, in private as well as public agencies.
 The BEST argument in support of such a merger is that

25._____

A. families with child care problems would not be broken up through placement of children
B. the taxpayer's and the voluntary contributor's money would be saved
C. through intensive work with children, prevention of the development of behavior problems would be possible
D. new techniques in family casework treatment and the development of new community resources would probably result

26. Family casework involves working with parents and children about problems involving maintenance and survival.
Of the following types of problems, the MOST important one that a family caseworker has to handle generally involves

   A. relationships between siblings
   B. budgeting
   C. psychotherapeutic problems
   D. environmental deficiencies

27. The authoritative approach in casework, also known as aggressive casework, essentially involves

   A. the breakup of families whose members no longer get along together
   B. purposeful, persistent casework methods observing respect for the individual
   C. direct supervision of a family until their problems are resolved
   D. the application of techniques evolved by law enforcement agencies to social casework

28. The term ambivalence, as used in social casework, might BEST be illustrated by the

   A. inability of the client to follow the recommendations of the caseworker, due to his own unresolved conflicts
   B. presentation to the client of more than one reasonable course of action for the client to follow
   C. client's lack of any knowledge of how to solve his problem
   D. client's fears for his future welfare

29. There is general agreement among experts in the field that, when dealing with a client or handling a case, a caseworker should

   A. place emphasis on the objective aspects, directing her work primarily to the physical factors in the client that indicate need for change
   B. place emphasis on the environmental factors, especially those surrounding the client which have caused him to be in his present state
   C. give attention not only to the environmental factors and social experiences, but also the client's feelings about, and reactions to, his experience
   D. consider each factor in the case as a separate unit after carefully distinguishing between the truly environmental and the truly emotional factors

30. In casework practice, the unit of attention is generally considered to be the family, although in some agencies the client or patient is often viewed as being outside of his family.
The trend in modern casework with respect to the family of a client is to

A. involve the family wherever feasible in the total casework process
B. scientifically determine wherein the family is harmful to the client and try to make plans for the client to leave his family
C. educate the public so that families of clients will not interfere with agency plans
D. refer every member of the family for casework help

31. John L., 15, was referred to a youth counseling agency by the principal of the high school he attends because he has been truanting for the past six months. He is of above average intelligence, is in his sophomore year, and is currently failing 4 out of 5 of his courses. His mother says that he frequently comes home after midnight and is friendly with two boys with court records. The family group consists of John and his mother, who supports them by working as a secretary. The sisters, 19 and 21, are married and out of the home. Mr. L. deserted when John was 3. The principal told John he had to go to the youth counseling agency or be brought into court by the truant officer.
In beginning to work with John, the caseworker should FIRST

31.____

A. recognize that since John did not come voluntarily, he will refuse casework treatment
B. establish himself as an adult who will keep John in line
C. secure more facts about John and his situation in order to determine further case activity
D. promise that the agency will keep John from being sent to juvenile court

32. A client tells the social worker that he is planning to leave his job as a junior executive trainee in a department store for a job as a laborer which will pay him a higher salary. After exploring the client's reasons for making this move, the caseworker feels the plan is unwise since the trainee position offers a considerably better future.
In this situation, it would be BEST for the caseworker to

32.____

A. attempt to dissuade the client from making the job change, pointing out the reasons for the inadvisability of the move
B. allow the client to change jobs, without attempting to dissuade or counsel him
C. refuse to give the client permission to change jobs, without an attempt to dissuade or counsel him
D. try to dissuade the client from making the job change without giving the real reasons for thinking the move undesirable

33. Casework interviewing is always directed to the client and his situation.
The one of the following which is the MOST accurate statement with respect to the proper focus of an interview is that the

33.____

A. caseworker limits the client to concentration on objective data
B. client is generally permitted to talk about facts and feelings with no direction from the caseworker
C. main focus in casework interviews is on feelings rather than facts
D. caseworker is responsible for helping the client focus on any material which seems to be related to his problems or difficulties

34. A recent development in casework interviewing procedure, known as multiple-client interviewing, consists of interviews of the entire family at the same time. However, this may not be an effective casework method in certain situations.
Of the following, the situation in which the standard individual interview would be PREFERABLE is when

   A. family members derive consistent and major gratification from assisting each other in their destructive responses
   B. there is a crucial family conflict to which the members are reacting
   C. the family is overwhelmed by interpersonal anxieties which have not been explored
   D. the worker wants to determine the pattern of family interaction to further his diagnostic understanding

35. The one of the following which is the CHIEF value of verbatim recording of all or a portion of an important interview is the possibility it offers for

   A. careful study and clarification of psychological goals in treatment
   B. a prompt solution to the problem by preservation, in an orderly and concise fashion, of the full psychological and economic picture of the client's situation
   C. quick determination of the more obvious social goals and offering of concrete services by presentation of the essential facts
   D. supervision of experienced workers by showing the emotional overtones, subtle reactions, and intricate worker-client interchanges

36. Experts in the field of social casework recording generally agree that the kind of case material for which the narrative form of recording is MOST suitable is

   A. material that deals with feelings, attitudes, and client-worker relationships because this style permits the use of primary evidence in the form of verbal material and behavior observed in the interview
   B. social data, including eligibility material and family background history, because it can then be presented in a chronological, orderly fashion to enable the worker to select the desired facts
   C. personal facts concerning the individual's personality patterns and their growth and development because they can be seen in an orderly progression from primal immaturity until their ultimate stage of completion
   D. selectively chosen and documented material essential to a quicker and clearer understanding of the various ramifications of the case by a new worker, when responsibility for handling the client is reassigned

37. A case record includes relevant social and psychological facts about the client, the nature of his request, his feeling about his situation, his attitude towards the agency, and his use of and reaction to treatment.
In addition, it should ALWAYS contain

   A. routine history
   B. complete details of personality development and emotional relationships
   C. detailed process accounts of all contacts
   D. data necessary for understanding the problem and the factors important in arriving at a solution

38. The CHIEF basis for the inability of a troubled client to express his problem clearly to the caseworker is that the client   38.____

    A. sees his problem in complex terms and does not think it possible to give the caseworker the whole picture
    B. has erected defenses against emotions that seem to him inadmissible or intolerable
    C. cannot describe how he feels about his problem
    D. views the situation as unlikely to be solved and is blocked in self-expression

39. During his pre-sentence investigation, a defendant gave information about his participation in the offense which conflicted with the official version. He was placed on probation. Now the district attorney wishes to use him as a witness against a co-defendant and asks for permission to use the pre-sentence report as a basis for cross-examination.
    Of the following, the BEST course of action to take is to   39.____

    A. refuse to turn over the report on the ground that the report is the property of the court and its contents cannot be revealed without authority of the court
    B. turn over the report to the district attorney but caution him to hold the source of his information confidential
    C. refer the request to the Director of Probation on the ground that this involves policy which no one else is ever authorized to handle
    D. advise the district attorney's office that the entire report cannot be sent to him but portions of it may be discussed with his representative

40. During the course of a pre-sentence investigation, the defendant reveals certain details of the offense not previously known and involves others who have not been apprehended.
    Of the following, the FIRST action to be taken by the probation officer on the case is to   40.____

    A. discuss the matter with the chief probation officer, asking guidance on methods of procedure
    B. report the new information to the district attorney's office immediately
    C. withhold the information until it can be disclosed to the court through the pre-sentence report in order to let the court decide how it is to be used
    D. advise the client of the importance of this information and ask him if he is prepared to make the same disclosures to the district attorney

41. A young man on probation after an offense involving fraudulent checks and impersonation of an officer is given work at a hospital as an attendant. Within three weeks, he marries a nurse's aide. A full investigation discloses that he told her he was wealthy, of good family, working humbly to *prove* himself.
    Of the following, the FIRST action for the probation officer to take in this case is to   41.____

    A. secure a warrant and cause his arrest immediately
    B. check with the hospital to get other details
    C. attempt to analyze the behavior pattern for causative factors
    D. recommend that the young couple get an annulment

42. The wife of a former probationer telephones the probation office stating that her husband has disappeared and she is anxious to secure all possible leads in order to aid the police in looking for him.
    Of the following, the BEST reply to be made to her is that   42.____

A. this is a job for the police, but if there are any developments, she will be informed
B. the case is closed and no help can be given her
C. she should consult her religious advisor and her attorney
D. the husband has had numerous previous girlfriends to whom he might have returned

43. A person of foreign birth is placed on probation but understands little English and cannot read or write. Of the following, the MOST appropriate action is to

   A. order him to attend night classes in English
   B. direct him to obtain someone who speaks his language to interpret the condition of probation
   C. encourage him to seek language training and tell him that his probation will be revoked if he shows unwillingness to overcome his language handicap
   D. give him guidance in finding a language class which will fit his needs and situation

44. The probation officer who made the pre-sentence investigation on a certain case happens to be personally acquainted with the judge who imposed sentence. Some time later, the judge receives a letter from the sentenced prisoner. The judge asks the probation officer to investigate this letter and make a recommendation.
Of the following, the BEST action for the probation officer to take is to

   A. make the investigation and report directly to the judge
   B. ask the judge to speak to his superior about this assignment
   C. complete the report and submit it to his superior for approval without prior consultation with the latter
   D. report to his superior that he has had a request for a supplementary investigation and await his decision as to whether it should be assigned to him or another officer

45. Having read another agency's record for information, it is GOOD case reporting practice to

   A. quote the agency worker as the source of information and include any pertinent opinions given in the agency file
   B. identify the source and report it over your signature as a part of the record
   C. use the words *it is alleged* or *according to a reliable source* or *we have been informed*
   D. refer to the other agency as Confidential Source No. 1, etc.

46. The type of pre-sentence report which is of GREATEST value is one which contains

   A. a diagnostic interpretation of the etiology of the offense
   B. the essential facts and indicates the treatment needs of the defendant
   C. the essential facts about the defendant
   D. a supplemental psychiatric study

47. The LEAST important reason for a probation officer to make a pre-sentence investigation and report is to

   A. assist the judge in making proper disposition of the case
   B. find conditions within the family which need the services of other agencies

C. assist the probation officer who will supervise the defendant if he is placed on probation
D. provide a case record for the institution if the defendant is committed

48. The one of the following statements which is MOST accurate in regard to violation of probation is that a violator should be returned to court

    A. only if he is guilty of a serious violation
    B. if further use of the authority of the court will have a therapeutic value in the case
    C. only if his detention is necessary for community production
    D. if commitment to a correctional institution had been under consideration before he was placed on probation

49. In dealing with violations of probation which have resulted in arrest, the probation officer should FIRST

    A. arrange for an immediate hearing before the sentencing judge in the original case
    B. discuss and evaluate the new violation with the arresting officer
    C. place a detainer against the probationer
    D. secure a voluntary statement from the probationer, including mention of his guilt or innocence

50. A probation officer sees a man on the street whom he believes is being sought under warrant as a probation violator. The probationer is not under his supervision. Of the following, the FIRST action the probation officer should take is to

    A. identify himself to the man and attempt to determine the latter's identity
    B. warn the probationer and report to his office that he has seen the violator
    C. advise the probationer to give himself up
    D. immediately contact the probation officer who has been supervising this probationer

## KEY (CORRECT ANSWERS)

| | | | | |
|---|---|---|---|---|
| 1. B | 11. A | 21. A | 31. C | 41. C |
| 2. D | 12. D | 22. A | 32. A | 42. A |
| 3. B | 13. B | 23. D | 33. D | 43. D |
| 4. A | 14. C | 24. C | 34. A | 44. D |
| 5. C | 15. D | 25. D | 35. A | 45. B |
| 6. C | 16. A | 26. D | 36. A | 46. B |
| 7. B | 17. D | 27. B | 37. D | 47. B |
| 8. D | 18. D | 28. A | 38. B | 48. B |
| 9. B | 19. C | 29. C | 39. A | 49. B |
| 10. C | 20. C | 30. A | 40. D | 50. A |

# EXAMINATION SECTION
# TEST 1

DIRECTIONS: Each question or incomplete statement is followed by several suggested answers or completions. Select the one that BEST answers the question or completes the statement. *PRINT THE LETTER OF THE CORRECT ANSWER IN THE SPACE AT THE RIGHT.*

1. Assume that you are conducting an initial interview with a married couple, both much younger than yourself, who are low-income people with very little formal education. As the husband's supervising probation officer, it would be MOST appropriate for you to address them as (or by)

    A. their first names, since this is how they are accustomed to being addressed
    B. *Mr.* and *Mrs.* and their last name, since this is a sign of seriousness and sincerity
    C. the husband's last name and the wife's first name, since this is the traditional manner in this couple's social group
    D. *sir* and *madam,* to emphasize the formality of the situation

1.____

2. In addition to other identifying data, the face sheet of a pre-sentence report should contain information relative to a defendant's age and marital status. Which of the following is the MOST appropriate entry which should be included on the face sheet of a pre-sentence report?
Age -

    A. 35, Marital status - divorced, 3/6/14
    B. 35, Born - 7/12/79, Marital status - divorced
    C. 35, Marital status - divorced, 3/6/14, expected to remarry 9/15
    D. 35, Born - 7/12/79, Marital status - divorced, 3/6/14, mental cruelty

2.____

3. Which one of the following statements BEST describes the proper scope of information about a defendant's numerous brothers and sisters which should be included in a pre-sentence report?

    A. Complete listing of names, dates of birth, occupations and residences by city and state of all brothers and sisters
    B. A listing of names, dates of birth, occupations, and residences by city and state of the brothers and sisters who might influence the defendant if placed on probation
    C. Data as stated in option A and a narrative summary on those who have had or are likely to have an influence on the defendant
    D. A narrative summary on only those brothers and sisters likely to have a positive or negative influence on the defendant if placed on probation

3.____

4. Assume that you are preparing a pre-sentence report. Two pieces of related information have come to your attention, in addition to the routine listing of arrests and convictions. The first piece of information comes from the police, who inform you that they have had strong reason to suspect your defendant of other offenses, but could never obtain enough evidence to arrest the defendant. The source of the second piece of information is a neighbor, who tells you, in confidence, that he witnessed the defendant cheat and steal from merchants, and get into fights, but no actual arrests were made. These offenses occurred at a different time from the offenses referred to by the police. Which of

4.____

21

these additional pieces of information, if any, should be included in your pre-sentence report?

    A. The first *only*  
    B. The second *only*  
    C. Both  
    D. Neither

5. Assume that you are gathering data for a pre-sentence report on a 21-year-old defendant. You have learned as a result of a visit to his high school that the defendant had severe serious emotional problems during the last half of his senior year.
The MOST appropriate of the following sections of your report in which to include this information is the section on

    A. psychological health  
    B. physical health  
    C. education  
    D. medical history

6. A psychiatrist's diagnosis of a defendant's mental health should be presented in a pre-sentence investigation report in the form of a(n)

    A. paraphrase of the psychiatrist's statements, using layman's terminology  
    B. interpretation by the probation officer of the psychiatrist's evaluation  
    C. direct quotation of the psychiatrist's diagnosis  
    D. statement by the probation officer appraising the defendant's mental health

7. Which one of the following is NOT a purpose of the pre-sentence investigation report?
To

    A. aid the court in sentencing the defendant  
    B. determine the guilt or innocence of the defendant  
    C. assist eventually in planning for release of the defendant  
    D. provide data for research in the field of criminal justice

8. Sexual conduct, may be a difficult and often embarrassing subject to investigate and report on.
Which one of the following statements BEST describes the scope of information which should be included in a pre-sentence report concerning a sexual offense?

    A. Terms such as *rape* or *sexual perversion* should be used in lieu of more explicit details, as these are universally understood and usually suffice.  
    B. Sexual acts should be described explicitly to give a clear, objective account of what transpired, including both parties' versions.  
    C. The defendant's version should be included, but the victim's testimony ommitted, since it is usually too embarrassing to elicit.  
    D. The information should be limited to that contained in the charges or indictment, as the participants' versions are usually subjective and misleading.

9. In preparing a pre-sentence report, of the following, a probation officer should place PRIMARY emphasis on

    A. major events in the life of the offender from birth  
    B. the meaning the offender has derived from his life experiences  
    C. the psychological profile of the offender  
    D. a chronological history of all circumstances leading to the offender's arrest and conviction

3 (#1)

10. The PRIMARY purpose of a pre-sentence investigation report by a probation officer is to

   A. serve as a future plan of treatment for the offender
   B. assist the court in making an appropriate disposition of a case
   C. protect society from the offender
   D. protect the offender's legal rights

11. In making a recommendation to the court on probation for an adult offender, of the following, the criterion that should generally be given the LEAST consideration is the

   A. protection of the community
   B. type of offense committed
   C. prospect of reforming the offender
   D. background of the offender

12. A pre-sentence investigation report usually includes a description of the offense committed by the defendant.
   Which one of the following sources would usually be considered LEAST reliable for this section of the report?

   A. The defendant
   B. Police records
   C. The complainant
   D. Eyewitnesses

13. Which one of the following types of information would MOST likely be found on a face sheet?

   A. Medical and mental examination reports
   B. Identifying data about the offender
   C. A synthesis of the case record
   D. Identifying data about the complainant

14. Assume that a probation officer has included a verbatim transcription of a probationer's indictment in his investigation report.
   This practice is GENERALLY considered

   A. *desirable*, mainly because inclusion of the indictment completes the picture of the probationer's situation
   B. *undesirable*, mainly because a transcript of the indictment is available to the court if needed
   C. *desirable*, mainly because inclusion of the document itself is the best guarantee of objectivity
   D. *undesirable*, mainly because the court already has knowledge of the indictment

15. The type of information about the client which is MORE essential in probation case records than in case records used in other fields of social work is

   A. an interpretation of the client and his situation
   B. accurate and easily available reference to verified facts about the client
   C. a running record of the progress of treatment
   D. a description of the client's attitude and reactions to his problems

16. A probation supervision case record generally includes all of the following EXCEPT

   A. contacts made with the probationer
   B. the probationer's personal and social situation

C. the probationer's progress in treatment
D. a copy of the original complaint

17. In writing case records, a probation officer should try to achieve a factual but interpretive report that gives a true picture of an individual and his situation. Which one of the following BEST describes the approximate proportions of factual and interpretive material which should be included in a typical case record?
   _____ factual; _____ interpretive.

   A. 10%; 90%   B. 20%; 80%   C. 50%; 50%   D. 90%; 10%

18. Which one of the following represents the MOST acceptable and desirable method of keeping case records?

   A. Records should include face sheets which are complete and constantly updated, with opening summary and periodic progress reports.
   B. Records should include full process recording and interpretation of the probation officer's thoughts and actions.
   C. A periodic summary recording should be prepared to show case movement, with detailed recording at crisis spots.
   D. Handwritten memoranda should be filed chronologically, covering the probationer's activities or the probation officer's reasoning at the time of writing.

19. A narrative record usually begins with a description of the complaint which brought the offender to the Department of Probation and continues with a relevant history of the case.
   Of the following, the MAIN advantage of organizing materials in this manner is that it

   A. indicates the basic reason why the offender is known to the criminal justice system
   B. gives the presiding judge all the facts before making a disposition of the case
   C. makes it easy for a new probation officer taking on the case in progress to learn all the facts readily
   D. fulfills the requirement that law enforcement agencies follow this procedure

20. Which one of the following should NOT be an integral part of a narrative record?

   A. A printed questionnaire, to record the probationer's responses and the probation officer's interpretive comments
   B. A flexible structure, to allow for the nature of the situation and individuality of the probation officer
   C. Records of interviews with the offender, family members, and witnesses to the offense
   D. The probation officer's interpretation of the individual and the situation involved

21. The part of the pre-sentence report prepared by a probation officer which is MOST helpful for diagnostic and treatment purposes is the

   A. face sheet               B. study of the offense
   C. arrest report            D. social case study

Questions 22-25.

DIRECTIONS: Questions 22 through 25 are to be answered SOLELY on the basis of the following statement.

The initial contact between the offender and the correctional social worker frequently occurs at the point of extreme crisis, when the usual adaptive mechanisms have been broken down. In many areas of correctional practice, such as probation and parole, this contact is often followed by long periods during which limited freedom is officially imposed. It is at such points that response to the offer of hope for restoring equilibrium may mean most, and that new coping capacities and new person-environment relationships develop. As a result, many correctional social workers have become skilled in strategies of crisis intervention. What they learn from such endeavors does not generally find its way into the professional literature; thus the correctional social worker has contributed little to developing and testing practice theory. However, beginning efforts are being made to remedy this situation, and it is probable that corrections may provide an important laboratory from which tomorrow's understanding of the theory and strategies of crisis intervention will emerge.

22. Which of the following is the MOST appropriate title for the above statement?

    A. Correctional Social Work in Crisis
    B. Crisis Intervention and Correctional Social Work
    C. Coping Capacities of Probationers and Parolees
    D. The Theory and Practice of Crisis Intervention

23. It can be concluded from the above statement that crisis intervention as a method of treatment and rehabilitation in correctional social work is based on the premise that a(n)

    A. offender may be more likely to respond to help and change his life style at a time of crisis, such as being on probation or parole, when incarceration is the only other alternative
    B. person is not likely to respond to help and change his life style unless he is in a crisis situation, such as being on probation or parole, when he is threatened by imprisonment
    C. offender sentenced to probation or parole is likely to respond to help and change his life style, because his freedom is limited and supervision is imposed on him
    D. situation such as probation or parole, in which an offender is supervised and his freedom is limited, presents ideal conditions for constructive personality change

24. On the basis of the above statement, it would be VALID to assume that

    A. offenders sentenced to probation and parole usually develop coping capacities which would not emerge during imprisonment
    B. offenders who are rehabilitated as a result of probation or parole have greater coping capacities in crisis situations
    C. a life crisis situation such as being sentenced to probation or parole may become a positive force toward an offender's rehabilitation
    D. an offender's ability to develop new coping capacities in times of crisis should be a decisive factor in determining the recommended sentence

25. According to the above statement, correctional social workers' experiences in crisis intervention have

    A. encouraged use of crisis intervention strategy
    B. contributed to theory rather than practice
    C. not resulted in further learning
    D. not generally been reported in print

## KEY (CORRECT ANSWERS)

1. B
2. B
3. C
4. C
5. A

6. C
7. B
8. B
9. B
10. B

11. B
12. A
13. B
14. B
15. B

16. D
17. C
18. C
19. A
20. A

21. D
22. B
23. A
24. C
25. D

# TEST 2

DIRECTIONS: Each question or incomplete statement is followed by several suggested answers or completions. Select the one that BEST answers the question or completes the statement. *PRINT THE LETTER OF THE CORRECT ANSWER IN THE SPACE AT THE RIGHT.*

1. Of the following letters written to a probation department in another jurisdiction, which one is written in the MOST acceptable style?

    A. This department wishes to acknowledge your communication of the 17th regarding your officers' efforts to locate John Jones. We wish to thank you for your efforts and ask you to return the warrant. Please be assured that we will cooperate with you should the occasion arise.
    B. This is in reply to your letter of May 17th, in which you advise that your officers have made an extensive search for John Jones, without success. Please accept our expression of appreciation for your services, and feel free to return the warrant. If we can ever render like service, feel free to call on us.
    C. This is in reply to your letter of May 17th. We want to thank you for your extensive efforts to find our fugitive, John Jones. You may return the warrant to us. If we can ever give similar assistance to your department, please do not hesitate to get in touch with us.
    D. Your letter of May 17th is herewith acknowledged. We note that your officers have made an extensive effort to locate John Jones, without finding him. We deem it advisable to terminate the search at present, and request you to return the warrant to us. We stand ready to accommodate you should you ever require our service in like circumstances

1.____

2. Assume that, as a probation officer, you are working on the police record section of a pre-sentence investigation report on an offender who has been arrested ten times in the last five years on various charges. Despite follow-up, however, you are unable to determine the disposition of half of these cases. The deadline for your report is the next day. Which one of the following courses of action would it be MOST appropriate for you to take with regard to preparing this section of your report? List

    A. all the arrests and only those dispositions of which you are aware, and leave a blank space for the unknown dispositions
    B. all the arrests and dispositions on cases of which you are aware, and fill in *no response from FBI* or other appropriate remarks on the cases whose dispositions are unknown
    C. none of the arrests and dispositions, but include instead an explanatory statement regarding the unavailability of complete disposition data
    D. only those arrests for which there are dispositions available, and make an explanatory statement to the effect that other arrests and dispositions will be added to the report when the information becomes available

2.____

3. For purposes of establishing rapport and obtaining information, the relative importance of an interviewer's overt behavior during an interview as compared to his underlying attitudes is such that the interviewer's overt behavior is GENERALLY considered

    A. dependent on the client's attitudes and behavior
    B. of equal importance

3.____

27

C. less important
D. more important

4. *Summary jurisdiction* is CORRECTLY defined as the

   A. authority of a court or magistrate to sentence defendants charged with minor offenses without indictment and usually without a jury
   B. action of a court or magistrate in cancelling or terminating a probationary period either to discharge or sentence the probationer
   C. recommittal of an accused person to custody after a partial or preliminary hearing before a judge or magistrate
   D. notice or order requiring a person to appear before a court for the purpose of being arraigned on the charge of committing an offense

5. It is considered advisable for the probation officer to classify his caseload according to the needs of his probationers and the kinds of service to be provided MAINLY because appropriate classification

   A. gives the judge a reliable indication of the seriousness of the offense and the offender's problems
   B. enables the probation officer to focus his attention and talents on areas of greatest need and potential productiveness
   C. makes it unnecessary for agency representatives and other professionals involved in the case to read all details of the case record
   D. indicates whether or not the probationer should be referred for psychiatric examination

6. The CHIEF distinction between a parolee and a probationer is that a parolee must have

   A. already served a part of his sentence in a penal or reformative institution before being released
   B. been placed on probation more than once within a 10-year period
   C. been convicted of a civil rather than a criminal offense
   D. been convicted of a felony rather than a misdemeanor

7. Children who have suffered from an attack of encephalitis sometimes become behavior problems or develop abnormal personality traits and are classified as psychoneurotic. If such a child becomes part of your caseload, you, as a probation officer, should know that generally the MOST effective type of treatment is

   A. probation         B. foster home placement
   C. penal             D. medical

8. A probation officer would use a clearance from a social service exchange PRIMARILY to obtain information on

   A. a probationer's family background, including police records
   B. a probationer's history of mental or physical treatment in public institutions
   C. any other agencies previously having contact with a probationer
   D. applications for public assistance by the probationer's family

9. In recommending a sentence of either probation or commitment to the court for a juvenile offender, the one of the following which should be taken into consideration LEAST by a probation officer is

A. the offender's potential for rehabilitation
B. social situations which can be utilized at home
C. the offender's pledges to behave in the future
D. social situations which can be utilized in the offender's school

10. The legal written document which initiates a case in Family Court is GENERALLY referred to as a(n)

    A. charge
    B. indictment
    C. petition
    D. information

11. Assume that you, as a probation officer, have an adolescent girl in your caseload, who is a recent runaway.
    Of the following, the service agency you should contact FIRST to help locate the runaway girl would be

    A. Travelers Aid Society
    B. Juvenile Protective Association
    C. YWCA
    D. Salvation Army

12. When an offender is sentenced to probation, this sentence generally should NOT be interpreted as a

    A. form of mercy or leniency
    B. contract between the offender and the court
    C. process of treatment prescribed by the court
    D. conditional release of the offender

13. Of the following, the MOST important reason for utilizing the intake procedure for juveniles in Family Court whenever possible is to

    A. save time for the Department of Probation staff
    B. satisfy the petitioner or complainant
    C. prevent the profound psychological effect on juveniles of a court visit
    D. enable parents of juveniles to have a greater voice in disposition of cases

14. Studies have shown that the correlation between a defendant's educational and vocational adjustment patterns and his emotional and social stability is USUALLY

    A. zero
    B. positive
    C. negative
    D. curvilinear

15. The one of the following which is NOT a responsibility of intake, as an integral part of the probation process, is to

    A. provide the opportunity for a satisfactory adjustment without court action
    B. refer cases to community agencies whenever the need for social services is indicated
    C. provide extended services if necessary in order to adjust cases satisfactorily
    D. refer to court only those cases that require court action

16. Recent newspaper articles have discussed proposed controversial legislation to change the minimum age at which a juvenile can be tried in criminal court instead of in family court.
    This proposed legislation is concerned SPECIFICALLY with _____ the age from _____.

    A. lowering; 16 to 14
    B. lowering; 18 to 16
    C. raising; 14 to 16
    D. raising; 16 to 18

17. A recent study of the results of compulsory and voluntary referrals of alcoholic probationers to psychotherapy indicates that those assigned to a compulsory treatment group had a more successful period of probation than those assigned to a voluntary treatment group. Probationers in compulsory treatment were in violation of probation for failure to attend a single treatment session, while those in the voluntary group were required to attend the first session only.
    These data suggest that, in general,

    A. compulsion may be a necessary factor for motivation and successful treatment of probationers
    B. initial motivation is a guarantee of successful treatment of probationers
    C. voluntary treatment of probationers results in decreased motivation
    D. successful treatment of probationers is directly related to their initial motivation to participate

18. For which one of the following crimes may a sentence of probation NOT be given in the state?

    A. Assault on a police officer
    B. Possession of a marijuana cigarette
    C. Grand larceny of over $100,000
    D. Possession of one ounce of heroin

19. Assume that one of your probationers appears for a scheduled appointment, admits that he is addicted to narcotics, and asks for help.
    As a probation officer, which one of the following would be the BEST action for you to take FIRST for both the probationer's well-being and the protection of society?

    A. Arrest the probationer for illegal use of narcotics and prepare a charge of violation of probation
    B. Arrange to refer the probationer to a suitable narcotics treatment resource for withdrawal treatment and further therapy and aftercare
    C. Refer the probationer to a methadone clinic
    D. Notify the Police Department Narcotics Squad

20. The practice of disclosing information contained in pre-sentence reports to adult defendants or their counsel is a controversial issue.
    Of the following, the argument against disclosing pre-sentence reports to defendants which is LEAST valid is that this practice would

    A. make it difficult for probation officers to obtain confidential information from other agencies
    B. cause unreasonable delays, since defendants are able to challenge information in the reports with which they disagree

C. be harmful to rehabilitative efforts, particularly in cases where psychiatric evaluations are included
D. reveal information about police techniques in apprehending criminal offenders

Questions 21-25.

DIRECTIONS: Questions 21 through 25 are to be answered SOLELY on the basis of the following statement.

The group worker must be concerned with two major goals in correctional treatment of juvenile offenders: (a) sustaining and reinforcing conventional value systems, and (b) enhancing the youth's positive self-image and general feeling of worthiness. The group processes involved in working toward these ends are so interrelated that treatment can meet both goals by improving interpersonal skills and experiences. As an initial concept, it is important to recognize that, in spite of delinquent behavior, adolescents usually do exhibit conscience formation, as may be seen in their support of conformity values, evidence of guilt and conventional behavior, and rationalization of delinquent behavior. It is this very ambivalence toward the conventional order that can be the basis for rehabilitation. On the basis of the distinction between real guilt and guilt reflecting emotional problems, an ideal therapeutic objective is to reach the point at which the internal and external controls are in general harmony and agency expectations are closely allied to and consistent with group and individual expectations.

21. Which of the following is the BEST title for the above statement?

    A. Group Treatment of Juvenile Offenders
    B. The Group Worker and Correctional Treatment
    C. The Juvenile Offender
    D. Conscience Formation in Juvenile Offenders

22. On the basis of the above statement, it would be VALID to assume that group treatment of the juvenile offender can result in the development of

    A. greater self-confidence
    B. rationalization of delinquent behavior
    C. guilt and conscience formation
    D. increased conscientiousness

23. On the basis of the above statement, it would be VALID to conclude that juvenile offenders

    A. are anxious for rehabilitation
    B. have no internal or external controls
    C. are deficient in interpersonal skills and experiences
    D. feel more guilt because of emotional problems than because of offenses committed

24. According to the above statement, a characteristic of juvenile offenders which makes them amenable to correctional treatment is that they

    A. can be reached by group processes
    B. have a general feeling of worthiness
    C. show signs of conscience formation
    D. are ambivalent toward rehabilitation

25. According to the above statement, an IDEAL therapeutic objective in the group treatment of juvenile offenders would be based on   25.____

    A. agency expectations
    B. group expectations
    C. the distinction between real guilt and irrational guilt
    D. the harmony between external and internal controls

## KEY (CORRECT ANSWERS)

| | |
|---|---|
| 1. C | 11. A |
| 2. B | 12. A |
| 3. D | 13. C |
| 4. A | 14. B |
| 5. B | 15. C |
| 6. A | 16. A |
| 7. D | 17. A |
| 8. C | 18. D |
| 9. C | 19. B |
| 10. C | 20. D |

21. A
22. A
23. C
24. C
25. C

#  EXAMINATION SECTION
## TEST 1

DIRECTIONS: Each question or incomplete statement is followed by several suggested answers or completions. Select the one that BEST answers the question or completes the statement. *PRINT THE LETTER OF THE CORRECT ANSWER IN THE SPACE AT THE RIGHT.*

1. Assume that, as a probation officer, you are assigned a pre-sentence investigation. In preparation for the initial interview with the defendant, you should FIRST

    A. send through a call sheet to the Department of Correction requesting that the defendant be produced for an interview
    B. secure a copy of the fingerprint report from the Police Department
    C. secure a copy of the indictment or criminal information from the District Attorney
    D. collect all available information about the defendant from the court docket, District Attorney file, police records, and report of offense

2. According to accepted practice, the probation officer explains the conditions of probation and the functions of the Department of Probation to the adult probationer during the initial interview.
Of the following, the CHIEF advantage of using this approach is that it

    A. serves as a convenient starting point in a new relationship
    B. places the new probationer on guard to avoid possible violations of probation
    C. eliminates the need to give the probationer written explanatory material
    D. assists in gaining the cooperation of the new probationer to help himself

3. Although an investigating probation officer may not be able to control the conditions under which he conducts an interview with a defendant or a collateral source of information, it is sometimes possible to select the site of the interview. Assume that a defendant is at liberty and it is necessary to secure information from him and from members of his family.
It would be PREFERABLE to

    A. set up an appointment for the defendant to see you at your office, scheduling a home visit later when the defendant is not at home
    B. set up a home visit where all members of the family, including the defendant, can be interviewed at once
    C. make a surprise home visit so the family and the defendant cannot *set the stage* for you in order to make a good impression
    D. call the defendant and the appropriate relatives into the office for a consecutive series of interviews, both individually and collectively

4. Assume that you are conducting an initial interview at a young probationer's home early in the evening. The mother of your client invites you to stay for dinner.
Of the following, your MOST appropriate response would be to

    A. *accept,* since it will give you an opportunity to become better acquainted with the probationer's family
    B. *decline,* explaining that you are not hungry, but tell the family you will be glad to stay for coffee
    C. *accept,* since refusal of the invitation might be construed as rejection
    D. *decline,* since acceptance of the invitation might interfere with performance of your professional role

5. Assume that you are supervising an adult probationer convicted of involuntary manslaughter, who is required to secure employment as a condition of probation. The probationer brings you an application given to him by a prospective employer, and asks you how much information he should divulge on the application with regard to his arrest, conviction, and probation.
As his supervising probation officer, you should instruct the probationer to

   A. leave that part of the application blank
   B. place an X in the arrest and convictions section, but give no other details
   C. include all the details, but explain that he has never been in trouble for stealing, since this is probably the employer's main concern
   D. fill out the application honestly and refer the employer to you if he has any further questions

6. Assume that a probation officer is interviewing a client who seems to be unable to hold a job for any length of time and has quit his most recent job after only two weeks.
In order to encourage the client to talk about this situation, of the following, it would be MOST appropriate for the probation officer to say,

   A. Did you quit that job because you weren't getting enough money?
   B. Tell me some of the reasons why you quit that job.
   C. Did your wife say anything when you quit that job?
   D. Well, I guess you will have to get busy and find another job.

7. A probation officer is interviewing a young male client who seems to be having difficulty describing how he got into his current life situation. When the probation officer asks him to tell his story, the client says,
*I am not sure if I can explain how I got into this mess.* Which of the following would be the probation officer's MOST appropriate response?

   A. Well, it may not be so important.
   B. Well, then, perhaps we can go on to something else.
   C. Well, we have very limited time.
   D. Well, tell it your own way and perhaps I can help you as you go along.

8. Assume that you are interviewing a new probationer for the first time. Initially, his answers to your routine questions are purposefully and continuously evasive and hostile.
In questioning this probationer further, the MOST appropriate of the following courses of action for you to take would be to

   A. refrain from responding to this provocative or *testing* behavior
   B. suggest that the interview be postponed until the probationer is ready to answer your questions in a forthright manner
   C. insist that the probationer tell you why he is being uncooperative
   D. warn the probationer that you will recommend a revocation of probation if he continues being evasive

9. To what extent should note-taking GENERALLY be used during an initial interview with a new probationer?

   A. All information the offender offers should be recorded.
   B. Essential confidential information only should be recorded.
   C. Notes should be taken on routine data only, and the remainder recorded later.
   D. Only information likely to be forgotten should be recorded.

10. Assume that a new probationer objects to certain rules and regulations concerning his conditions of probation.
    Of the following, the MOST effective way to handle these objections initially, while maintaining the probationer's active willing cooperation, is to

    A. explain that all probationers must comply with certain conditions and that the probation officer cannot modify or change them
    B. remind him that his probation might be revoked if he does not comply
    C. point out that compliance with probation conditions often results in early release from probation
    D. explore and evaluate his objections, while explaining the reasons for the rules and regulations

11. Assume that you are a probation officer interviewing a new probationer who is considerably older than you. Early in the interview, the probationer starts to reminisce about the *good old days.*
    You should consider this reminiscing on the part of the probationer to be

    A. *beneficial,* because it may have the effect of reducing the existing age difference, which could be a barrier to successful interviewing
    B. *harmful,* because the probationer has already been convicted and should stick to the subject of the discussion as you direct
    C. *beneficial,* because it may have the effect of eliminating guilt feelings the probationer might have about his crime
    D. *harmful,* because it may have a negative and depressing psychological effect on both you and the probationer

12. With regard to the chances of establishing a good relationship in an interview situation between a client and a probation officer of the same or opposite sex, studies have GENERALLY shown that

    A. there are fewer barriers between a male client and a female probation officer than between a female client and a male probation officer
    B. there are fewer barriers between a male client and a female probation officer than between a male client and a male probation officer
    C. the sex of the parties has no bearing on the information obtained or topics discussed
    D. there may be barriers due to the difference in sex, but they can usually be overcome by a skillful interviewer

13. As an investigating probation officer, you are interviewing the mother of a juvenile offender in the family's small apartment. The mother is confused and upset as a result of her son's difficulties and she has not been able to answer several essential questions satisfactorily. Your BEST course of action in this situation is to

    A. ask these questions again at the next interview when the mother should hopefully be less upset
    B. repeat these questions patiently until the necessary information is brought to light
    C. firmly impress upon the mother that you cannot terminate the interview until she has answered the questions
    D. refer the mother to a family agency where she can receive counseling for her problems about her son

14. Assume that you are a probation officer interviewing an adult defendant who is due for sentencing. Since the defendant was unable to post bail, the interview takes place in the defendant's cell, and the surroundings are physically uncomfortable.
    In order to put the defendant at ease and secure as much information as possible from him, it would be MOST helpful for you to

    A. talk in an authoritative voice to impress the defendant with the seriousness of his situation
    B. try to disregard the surroundings and appear relaxed, while focusing on the interview
    C. act in a businesslike manner and handle the interview as though you were in your office
    D. ask a fellow inmate to witness the interview, to make the defendant feel more comfortable

15. Which one of the following types of questions would generally be considered INEFFECTIVE during an interview with a defendant?

    A. Questions which require a *yes* or *no* answer
    B. Open-ended questions which require some explanation
    C. Questions that might be difficult for the defendant to answer
    D. Questions which have emotional connotations

16. It is generally agreed that, when verifying information given to you by a defendant, it is best to have the defendant's concurrence before checking with certain sources, such as a previous employer.
    If a defendant disagrees with your decision after you have explained your reason for considering a contact essential for your pre-sentence report, it would generally be MOST appropriate for you to

    A. contact the source despite the defendant's objection
    B. respect the defendant's wishes and not make the disputed contact
    C. ask the defendant to get the information for you in writing
    D. postpone the contact and try to convince the defendant to agree at a later date

17. Assume that, during the course of your pre-sentence investigation of a defendant, you find that the complainant, who was the defendant's victim, is guilty of contributing to the offense for which the defendant was convicted.
    In preparing your pre-sentence report relative to this finding, of the following, the BEST practice would be to

    A. include all significant information about the complainant's involvement
    B. omit any reference to the complainant's involvement
    C. make only a brief reference to the complainant's involvement
    D. give your interpretation of the complainant's motivation

18. It is generally considered appropriate for the probation officer to use non-directive, open questions during the early part of the interview with the probationer MAINLY because such questions

    A. allow the probationer to choose his own approach to the content of the question
    B. impose heavier demands on the probationer to tell his story fully
    C. help the probationer to select and organize his responses
    D. encourage responses that are factual and brief

19. In order to conduct a successful interview with a client, the probation officer must decide to what degree the interview should be structured and controlled.
    Of the following, the MOST likely effect of a highly structured interview is to

    A. provoke anxiety and hostility in the client
    B. lessen the client's confidence and cooperativeness
    C. reduce anxiety and increase the client's confidence
    D. violate the client's integrity and right of self-determination

20. The QUICKEST and MOST informative of the following methods of determining how a juvenile defendant relates to other members of his immediate family is to

    A. interview the defendant
    B. interview members of the defendant's immediate family
    C. have a staff psychologist administer projective tests to the defendant
    D. construct a sociogram of the immediate family

21. Assume that, during an interview with a young male client, a probation officer wants to change the subject under discussion and go back to another, more important topic which the client brought up earlier in the interview.
    In directing the discussion back to the earlier subject, it would be MOST advisable for the probation officer to

    A. comment on it without mentioning that the client was talking about the subject before, mainly because the client may realize that he was avoiding this topic and refuse to go back to it
    B. use the previous comments and, if possible, even the client's own words about the more important subject, mainly because this suggests that the probationer has shared responsibility for going back to it
    C. summarize in his own words the material just discussed by the client, mainly because this will help him to become aware that he has exhausted it and should go back to the other subject
    D. inform the client that he cannot avoid talking about the topic discussed earlier in the interview, mainly because this will make him aware of the importance of this subject

22. A common error made by inexperienced probation officers in their early interviews is to talk too much, and give the interviewee too little opportunity to talk.
    In order to listen effectively, the probation officer should do all of the following with the EXCEPTION of

    A. following what is being said overtly
    B. following the latent overtones of what is being said
    C. assuming that he knows what is going to be said
    D. acting relaxed but alert and attentive to what is said

23. Assume that a probation officer has received reports from a young female probationer's employer that she is not getting along with her fellow workers. During the weekly interview, the probation officer attempts to focus on this problem, but the probationer persistently digresses from the subject of her job.
In this situation, of the following, it would be MOST appropriate for the probation officer to say

   A. That's interesting, and perhaps we can come back to it later. However, it may be more helpful if we could talk about the way you get along on your job.
   B. Now, let's not change the subject. Your boss tells me you're not getting along with the people at work and you will be in trouble if you get yourself fired.
   C. You're changing the subject because you don't want to talk about your job. That's the important thing right now, and we can't waste time discussing anything else.
   D. You know, I have six more interviews today, and I only have time to discuss things that might affect your probation. So let's get back to talking about the trouble on your job.

24. In considering the use of religion to assist the probationer, the probation officer should

   A. include church attendance as a prerequisite in the treatment plan
   B. not try to develop a religious connection through the use of his legal authority
   C. require the probationer to attend church for a trial period
   D. never use religion as a community resource or as a subject of discussion with the probationer

25. Assume that a probation officer has learned that a young male probationer under his supervision is not following the instructions of the court about his recreational activities, and has been associating with his former companions at a pool hall which has a bad reputation.
At the next interview, of the following actions, it would be MOST advisable for the probation officer to

   A. tell the probationer that he has violated probation and warn him that he will be penalized if he does not obey the court
   B. tell the probationer that he is aware of his activities, and that he plans to watch him more closely in the future
   C. try to get the probationer to discuss his feelings about his companions, his interests, and his recreational activities
   D. avoid discussing the probationer's leisure time activities unless he brings up the subject himself

# KEY (CORRECT ANSWERS)

1. D
2. A
3. A
4. D
5. D

6. B
7. D
8. A
9. C
10. D

11. A
12. D
13. B
14. B
15. A

16. A
17. A
18. A
19. C
20. C

21. B
22. C
23. A
24. B
25. C

---

# TEST 2

DIRECTIONS: Each question or incomplete statement is followed by several suggested answers or completions. Select the one that BEST answers the question or completes the statement. *PRINT THE LETTER OF THE CORRECT ANSWER IN THE SPACE AT THE RIGHT.*

1. Assume that a probation officer is interviewing a female juvenile offender who is being sent to a residential treatment center by order of the court. During the interview, she tells the probation officer that she will do her best to escape soon after she arrives at the center. The BEST course of action for the probation officer to take would be to   1.____

    A. advise the girl that she will be committed to a state training school if she tries to escape
    B. accept the girl's statement as part of her total behavior, but tell her that you will share this information with the treatment center
    C. pay no attention to the girl's statement and allow the treatment center to handle her attempts to escape
    D. ignore the girl's statement since escaping from the treatment center will be much more difficult than she thinks

2. The one of the following which is generally considered to be the MOST important factor in the selection of probation as an alternative to institutionalization is the offender's   2.____

    A. age
    B. motivation for adjustment
    C. family relationships
    D. history of arrests

3. The suggestion has been made that probation agencies, like many private casework agencies, should adopt the practice of charging a modest fee for probation service. Of the following, the MOST valid reason why this practice could serve a useful purpose is that   3.____

    A. probationers would have additional pressure to earn a living by legitimate means
    B. fee payment would give the probationer an opportunity to meet his financial responsibilities
    C. fees collected from probationers would make a substantial contribution to public funds
    D. payment of a modest fee would help the probationer maintain his self-respect and do his best to benefit from probation

4. Which of the following is the MOST important reason why the rules and regulations applying to probation facilitate rehabilitation of the probationer?
The   4.____

    A. probationer can derive emotional security from knowing, *I can go so far, but no further*
    B. probation officer can base his authority on statutes established by his department
    C. probationer can be penalized for infractions without being referred back to court
    D. probation officer can refer to a clear statement of the functions and aims of probation

5. Experts generally believe that rules and regulations applying to probationers are MOST useful when they are   5.____

A. adapted uniformly to all probationers
B. adapted to the needs of the given individual and to the conditions
C. expressed in negative rather than positive terms
D. phrased in positive terms even when they are not always rigidly enforced

6. Assume that during the course of a pre-sentence investigation you receive a telephone call from the brother of a defendant, asking you to visit him at his place of business, a women's coat factory, with regard to his brother's case. During the visit, the defendant's brother offers to give you a *good price* on a new coat for your wife.
Of the following responses, it would be MOST appropriate for the probation officer to

   A. *refuse,* because your pre-sentence report on the defendant may be unfavorable
   B. *accept,* because the coat is not offered as an outright gift
   C. *refuse,* since the brother's offer may be construed as an attempt to influence the nature of the pre-sentence report
   D. *accept,* since you will be able to make a note of this offer in the case record, which is submitted to the court

7. In the city, probation work is divided into three phases or points in the legal process, which include

   A. investigation, supervision, and correction
   B. intake, supervision, and reporting
   C. supervision, correction, and intake
   D. intake, investigation, and supervision

8. Of the following, an investigating probation officer assigned to conduct a pre-sentence investigation for the court is MAINLY responsible for

   A. developing a full story of the offense and the defendant's participation so that the judge can impose appropriate punishment
   B. convincing the defendant that he has done wrong and is about to receive just punishment for his crime
   C. providing the court with an account of the defendant's participation in the crime, motivation, and previous life style
   D. recommending to the court what he believes to be an appropriate disposition of the case

9. Assume that a probation officer has determined that one of his probationers, who is not psychotic, requires psychiatric treatment.
Of the following, the MOST appropriate action for the probation officer to take is to

   A. refer the probationer to a psychiatric treatment center and order him to make an appointment
   B. interpret to the probationer his need for psychiatric therapy in an effort to have him take the initiative in entering treatment
   C. make an appointment at a psychiatric treatment center for the probationer and accompany him to the first visit
   D. stipulate to the probationer that his acceptance of psychiatric treatment will be a condition of probation

10. Assume that, during the course of a pre-sentence investigation, you, as a probation officer, make a pre-arranged visit to an offender's residence to obtain a clear picture of the way he lives. In addition to the offender, family members are also present. Statements made by family members in response to your questions should GENERALLY be considered to be LACKING in

    A. vindictiveness
    B. protectiveness
    C. bias
    D. objectivity

11. Suppose you are interviewing a male defendant for the purpose of preparing a pre-sentence investigation report. Based on what he has told you so far, you believe that his chances for probation are good. A little later in the interview, the defendant expresses concern for his wife's ability to support herself and their three children if he is sentenced to a jail term.
    Of the following, your BEST initial response to the defendant's concern would be as follows:

    A. Why didn't you consider this possibility before you committed the offense?
    B. You're right. It won't be easy to manage, but help may be available to her if she is in need.
    C. Don't worry. Everything will be all right.
    D. Based on what you've told me, your chances for probation are good.

12. Authorities in the field of probation generally emphasize the concept that it is essential for the probation officer to have an accepting, nonjudgmental attitude in order to maintain a positive and helpful relationship with his clients.
    Of the following, the MOST valid description of this concept is that the probation officer

    A. is concerned with understanding, rather than praising or blaming the client
    B. agrees with the client's point of view and his concept of reality
    C. resists making generalizations about the client
    D. communicates confidence in the client's ability to direct his own life

13. Assume that, during a conference with his supervisor, a newly appointed probation officer expresses concern because he feels antagonistic and anxious in the presence of one of his clients, and these feelings tend to cause problems during the interview.
    The supervisor suggests that this may be due to counter-transference, a psychological concept which means that negative feelings are activated because the probation officer

    A. overidentifies with the client and his difficulties
    B. associates the client with some significant person in his own past
    C. has a preconceived judgment about the client's ethnic group
    D. believes that the client is hostile and angry with him

14. The interviewing technique called *clarification* would be PROPERLY used by a probation officer in counseling a probationer who

    A. has trouble verbalizing his feelings
    B. requires reassurance and encouragement
    C. is confused about the significance of his thoughts
    D. needs discipline and firm treatment

15. According to accepted practice, in preparing a pre-sentence investigation report it is considered advisable for the probation officer to interview the complainant, MAINLY because the complainant is likely to

   A. give the most objective account of the crime
   B. be the primary source of information about the crime
   C. have been a participant in the crime
   D. suggest the most suitable sentence for the crime

16. Assume that you have made an appointment for a 3 P.M. home visit to a female probationer with a young child, but find that you will be delayed about an hour by a backlog of interviews in your office.
   In this situation, it would be MOST advisable to

   A. telephone the probationer and ask her to see you in your office the next morning instead
   B. visit the probationer an hour later than the scheduled appointment, without phoning first
   C. telephone the probationer as soon as you know you will be delayed and tell her that you will be about an hour late
   D. cancel your present appointment by telephone and make another appointment for the next week

17. Assume that a probation officer is aware that a client, who is an alcoholic, has been lying to him about participating in drinking sessions during the previous week. During the interview, it would be ADVISABLE for the probation officer to _____ the client says, mainly because the _____.

   A. *accept;* probation officer will jeopardize his relationship with the client if he questions the client's veracity
   B. *question;* probation officer would not be able to use his authority effectively to help the client if he accepts the lie
   C. *accept;* client will lose confidence in the probation officer if he questions the lie
   D. *question;* client may think he is ready for discharge from probation if the probation officer accepts the lie

18. Assume that, as a probation officer, you are conducting a supervision interview with a juvenile offender who acts cocky, and deliberately makes provoking remarks. Finally, he says, *you people can't do a thing to me because I've been here before and I know my rights as a juvenile.* Of the following, your BEST reaction to this attitude and behavior would be to say:

   A. I can understand how you feel, but wouldn't you like to tell me why you seem to be so angry?
   B. If you know what's good for you, you'll cooperate with me, because you may not get away so easily this time.
   C. Your rights may be important to you, but the rights of society must also be protected.
   D. You're absolutely correct, but I'm getting paid to try to rehabilitate you, if at all possible.

19. Assume that an emotional topic is being discussed with a probation officer during the course of an interview with a defendant, and the defendant stops talking suddenly. A 30-second silence follows.
    In this situation, of the following, it is usually MOST important for the probation officer to

    A. try to understand the meaning of the silence and respond accordingly
    B. ask another question on the subject being discussed
    C. ask a question about a new subject
    D. talk about his own experiences regarding the subject under discussion

20. It is important for the probation officer to recognize and understand a client's feelings of ambivalence.
    The behavioral manifestation of ambivalence that appears MOST frequently in the probation interview is

    A. timidity
    B. indecision
    C. arrogance
    D. hostility

21. Studies have confirmed that race and sex differences between interviewer and interviewee present inherent barriers to effective interviewing, varying in degree. The MOST potentially problematic of the following combinations is a _____ client interviewed by a _____ probation officer.

    A. black male; black female
    B. white female; white male
    C. black male; white female
    D. white female; black female

22. Assume that one of your cases is a middle-aged Puerto Rican woman whose period of probation is almost completed. She speaks very little English, and you have not been able to motivate her to attend the night school English classes which you have recommended. However, she is steadily employed as a seamstress, does not need English on her job or in her predominantly Spanish neighborhood, and has otherwise made a satisfactory adjustment within her limitations.
    Of the following, the MOST appropriate course of action for you to take to benefit this probationer would be to

    A. suggest to your supervisor that she be transferred to a Spanish-speaking probation officer
    B. recommend discharge when her period of probation is over
    C. report her to the court for failure to attend English classes
    D. offer her an early discharge from probation if she attends English classes

23. Sociotherapy, a highly effective technique especially useful for persons with limited expressive ability, is distinguished from psychotherapy in that sociotherapy deals MAINLY with

    A. changing a client's ability to cope with a situation
    B. changing a situation so that it is easier to handle
    C. restructuring the client's basic attitudes toward social institutions
    D. developing a theoretical Utopian social status the client can strive to achieve

24. During an interview with a probationer of low income and education levels, to facilitate understanding your questions should GENERALLY be formulated so as to focus on which of the following types of information?

    A. Abstract details
    B. Symbolic activities
    C. Concrete situations
    D. Introspective matters

25. In order for a middle-class, white probation officer to conduct a meaningful, successful interview with a lower class, black probationer, the probation officer's manner of speaking should be

    A. the same as his usual manner, but include colloquialisms such as *jive* and *rap*
    B. the same as his usual manner when talking to a layman or any other probationer
    C. different from his usual manner in that he should use simpler language
    D. different from his usual manner in that he should be more formal

---

# KEY (CORRECT ANSWERS)

| | | | |
|---|---|---|---|
| 1. | B | 11. | B |
| 2. | B | 12. | A |
| 3. | D | 13. | B |
| 4. | A | 14. | C |
| 5. | B | 15. | B |
| 6. | C | 16. | C |
| 7. | D | 17. | B |
| 8. | C | 18. | A |
| 9. | B | 19. | A |
| 10. | D | 20. | B |

21. C
22. B
23. B
24. C
25. B

# EXAMINATION SECTION
# TEST 1

DIRECTIONS: Each question or incomplete statement is followed by several suggested answers or completions. Select the one that BEST answers the question or completes the statement. *PRINT THE LETTER OF THE CORRECT ANSWER IN THE SPACE AT THE RIGHT.*

1. One of the earliest of the names associated with the probation movement is

    A. Homer Folks
    B. Ben Lindsey
    C. Helen D. Pigeon
    D. John Augustus

2. Of the following, the fundamental theory of probation rests MOST NEARLY on

    A. the fear of punishment
    B. exercise by the court of its power of compulsion
    C. a promise by the offender to better his ways
    D. the frequency of recidivism

3. Release of offenders under supervision as an alternative to punishment was FIRST developed as a legal system in

    A. Ancient Rome
    B. France
    C. the United States
    D. Great Britain

4. The social agency conducting an institution for the care and treatment of delinquent and emotionally disturbed boys, which was founded originally for the care of Black children only, is the

    A. Wiltwyck School
    B. Vanderbilt Clinic
    C. Craig Colony
    D. Claremont House

5. A probation officer encountering a reference to *prognosis* in a case report would MOST accurately associate the term with

    A. a casual relationship
    B. psychosis
    C. a congenital disease
    D. a forecast

6. A probation report which describes a youngster as perspicacious seeks to convey the impression to the reader that the youngster is

    A. loquacious
    B. clever
    C. shrewish
    D. garrulous

7. In reporting on a person who thinks he sees objects which are NOT present and may NOT be real, the probation officer should describe such an individual as having

    A. claustrophobia
    B. delusions
    C. hallucinations
    D. paranoia

8. A good probation report should possess some of the following qualities, the LEAST desirable of which is

    A. legibility
    B. clarity
    C. coherence
    D. invalidity

9. When interviewing an individual with a reputation for being a conciliatory person, the probation officer should MOST reasonably expect to find that he

   A. is flippantly smooth
   B. has an appeasing manner
   C. is fickle
   D. has an uncontrollable temper

10. A juvenile whose veracity is frequently doubted is BEST described as

    A. a fabricator
    B. an alien
    C. born out of wedlock
    D. underprivileged

11. An adolescent who is habitually discontented could BEST be described as

    A. invidious
    B. plaintive
    C. quibbling
    D. captious

12. Siblings are MOST easily identified by

    A. blood
    B. adoption proceedings
    C. color
    D. speech

13. Occupational therapy is MOST closely associated with

    A. vocational guidance
    B. position classification
    C. curative handicraft
    D. diathermic treatment

14. Of the following degrees of deviation from normal mentality, the one indicating the LEAST intelligence is the

    A. moron
    B. imbecile
    C. idiot
    D. borderline

15. The person whose duty it is to manage the estate of a minor or of an incompetent is called the

    A. executor
    B. probate officer
    C. amicus curiae
    D. guardian

16. An order for a witness to appear in court is called

    A. a subpoena
    B. an injunction
    C. a mandamus
    D. res judicata

17. *Ostensibly a sane person, yet severely mentally ill and dangerous to himself and others* is a description MOST commonly applied to a

    A. psychopath
    B. paraplegic
    C. paretic
    D. paranoid

18. The impact upon society of mental disease is MOST adequately indicated by

    A. its responsibility for sex crimes and delinquency
    B. the phenomenal growth of feeble-mindedness in the United States
    C. the increasing number of deaths resulting from it
    D. the burden of its disabling effects on the community

19. A deficiency disease is a disorder caused by a(n)   19.____

    A. deficiency of medical aid
    B. diet lacking certain vitamins or minerals
    C. lack of proper rest and relaxation
    D. insufficient quantity of sugar in the diet

20. Delinquency on the part of a child is believed to result PRIMARILY from   20.____

    A. emotional and personality maladjustments
    B. environmental handicaps
    C. physical disability
    D. sociological factors

21. In determining whether or not an offender should be placed on probation, the MOST important factor for the probation officer to consider is the   21.____

    A. attitude of the community
    B. personality of the offender
    C. offense
    D. attitude of the court

22. A probation officer who has an objective attitude in social research would   22.____

    A. deal only with concrete reality rather than with abstract ideas
    B. use only evidence favorable to the objective
    C. object to all new hypotheses
    D. follow the evidence regardless of personal interests

23. In collecting social evidence from personnel in the public school system of the city, a probation officer would expect to find that the one of the following who makes the BEST social witness is the   23.____

    A. principal of the school at which the offender was a pupil
    B. superintendent of schools
    C. teacher who is able to individualize his pupils
    D. truant officer

24. The BEST of the following reporting techniques in releasing statistical data of a social nature is to publish   24.____

    A. percentage figures
    B. ratio figures
    C. absolute figures
    D. a descriptive summary without such figures

25. Progressively minded probation officers agree that the type of social treatment given a delinquent should be determined PRIMARILY by the   25.____

    A. nature of the offense committed
    B. type and variety of social problems causing the delinquency
    C. size of the probation officer's case load
    D. plan recommended by the judge

26. From a psychological point of view, delinquency can MOST accurately be considered as  26.___

   A. a definite congenital trait which causes inability to adjust to society
   B. overt acts which come into conflict with natural instincts
   C. a symptom of a deeper maladjustment which manifests itself in an inability to adjust to society
   D. none of the above

27. The TRUE extent of delinquency and crime in the United States is  27.___

   A. known accurately on an annual basis
   B. estimated on an annual basis
   C. known accurately in certain fields
   D. gathered statistically during each census year

28. The belief that crime can be prevented BEST by enforcing laws rigidly is based on the theory that  28.___

   A. persons cannot continue criminal careers as freely during periods of incarceration
   B. suppression leads to sublimation
   C. punishment is the most effective deterrent known against lawbreakers
   D. multiplicity of laws causes confusion in their attempted enforcement

29. Studies of penology reveal that punishment has  29.___

   A. seldom served as a crime deterrent
   B. successfully served as a crime deterrent
   C. served as a crime deterrent only in cases of larceny
   D. not served as a crime deterrent because the penalties inflicted have been too moderate

30. In the classifications of crime listed below, the one in which the probation officer would expect to find the HIGHEST proportion of arrests of females would be recorded in uniform crime reports under the heading of  30.___

   A. assault
   B. automobile theft
   C. burglary
   D. rape

31. A national magazine conducting a long-term feature devoted to techniques of crime prevention regularly prints contributions from such persons as an ex-president of the United States, a mayor, a congressman, a governor, and a civil court judge.
   A probation officer would MOST logically conclude from this example that  31.___

   A. there is as yet a great deal of inconclusive thinking on the causes of crime and the treatment of those causes
   B. public officials are better judges of the effectiveness of crime prevention techniques than persons not in the public service
   C. the experiences of sociologists and psychiatrists have been wholly negative in the field of crime prevention
   D. the best approach to crime prevention is that which encompasses the activities of local, state, and federal officials of every type

32. The PRIMARY reason for recording the results of a probation investigation is that the

    A. law requires that this be done
    B. written record is more impressive and credible than an oral report
    C. reader exerts a minimum of effort in comprehending and digesting the information
    D. data obtained may be made secretly and permanently available

33. According to studies conducted on methods of questioning during intake procedure by interviewers such as probation officers, a truthful statement of fact is LEAST easily obtained from the person being questioned if he is

    A. allowed to use an uninterrupted narrative form of expression
    B. cross-examined frequently by the person doing the interviewing
    C. encouraged to present his facts in chronological order
    D. interrupted as seldom as possible

34. The CHIEF concern of the pre-sentence investigation in a criminal court should be, according to the views expressed by the most noted researchers in the field of probation, to

    A. speed up the court procedures so that more cases can be handled expeditiously
    B. discover the immediate cause of the offender's being brought before the court
    C. determine whether the person brought before the court is innocent or guilty of the charges lodged against him
    D. explore all the social factors that have a bearing on the personality and behavior of the offender

35. To a probation officer, the ultimate object of a pre-sentence investigation is

    A. knowledge that will insure the punishment of the offender if a crime has been committed
    B. knowledge that will protect society from the criminal
    C. understanding of the offender from the point of view of his possible re-integration as a self-sufficient and permanently useful member of society
    D. understanding of the offender that will explain why he committed the crime and will enable society to guard against that sort of criminal activity

36. Case study procedure differs from statistical procedure MOST markedly in that

    A. the basis for statistical study is observation
    B. statistical procedure can be divided into inventory, analysis, and inference
    C. incorrect data in statistical procedure may result in an incomplete analysis
    D. statistical procedure has a broad numerical base making restriction of subjects necessary

37. Suppose that a good probation department were identified by each of the features listed below.
    If you, a probation officer, were studying the organization of such an agency, you would expect to find its correctional program LEAST affected by the removal of its

    A. enlightened policies
    B. trained and competent personnel
    C. suitable equipment and supplies with which to have its work done
    D. advisory board of the most notable penologists in the country

38. The one of the following which BEST expresses one of the fundamental foundations of the probation system is a(n)

    A. desire to reward the first offender in order to encourage good conduct
    B. desire to protect society by facilitating the readjustment of the probationer
    C. economy measure designed to save the government the cost of supporting prisoners in institutions
    D. growing attitude of leniency toward offenders

39. From the point of view of the probation officer, to integrate into normal groups children presenting symptoms of mild behavior disorder would be

    A. too radical a proposal; it has never been tried successfully
    B. impracticable; participation of problem children would jeopardize the program of the other children in the group
    C. undesirable; children otherwise emotionally stable would tend to become corrupted
    D. beneficial; it would expose the problem children to the beneficent effect of group activity with children possessing conforming behavior patterns

40. The detention of children waiting for a court decision as to whether they should be retained on a charge of having committed a minor offense is considered socially undesirable by progressively minded probation officers because the

    A. children may be cleared of the charge and, therefore, found to have been detained without cause
    B. children may be subjected to emotional damage
    C. parents may become unnecessarily concerned over the children's absence from home
    D. community is charged with the expense of lodging and feeding the children

41. Of the PRIMARY functions of a modern police department in dealing with juvenile delinquency, one should be to

    A. arrest the parents of delinquents and hold them responsible for neglecting their duties as parents
    B. perform social case work with the families of delinquent children
    C. recommend the level of treatment for children presenting behavior problems
    D. take an active part in programs designed to prevent juvenile delinquency

42. Legally, the BEST definition of juvenile delinquency is: Any child under

    A. 18 who has deserted his home and who habitually associates with dissolute, vicious, or immoral persons
    B. 16 who has violated a city ordinance or who has committed any offense, except murder or manslaughter, against the laws of the state
    C. 18 who has violated a city ordinance or who has committed any offense, except murder or manslaughter, against the laws of the state
    D. 16 who is habitually disobedient to the reasonable and lawful commands of his parents and who habitually absents himself from school or who persistently violates school regulations

43. Current interest in child guidance clinics was developed because of an increasing belief    43.____
that

    A. at least one-tenth of the nation's youth is destined to end in prison if not given systematic guidance
    B. children should be treated as miniature adults
    C. many of the emotional and mental disabilities of later life result from unfortunate childhood experiences
    D. the best interests of the nation require standardization of each child's education

44. A probationary sentence, such as the one given Joseph Buttafuoco for statutory rape of    44.____
Amy Fisher, has its PRIMARY effect in

    A. punishing the defendant
    B. deterring such acts
    C. showing the public that justice has been meted out
    D. allowing a defendant to plead guilty and walk

45. During a period of probation in which records were kept for 360 children fourteen to eighteen years of age, probation officers found that the group committed certain offenses, as shown in the following table:    45.____

    | I.Q. | No. of Offenders | No. of Offenses | Offenses Per Offender |
    |---|---|---|---|
    | 61-80 | 125 | 338 | 2.7 |
    | 81-100 | 160 | 448 | 2.8 |
    | 101 and over | 75 | 217 | 2.9 |

    According to the above data,
    A. the more intelligent offenders are no more law-abiding than, and perhaps not so law-abiding as, the dull offenders
    B. brighter offenders present no more difficult problems than less intelligent offenders
    C. the majority of this probation group is found to be above the average in intelligence of a normal group of young persons within this age range
    D. the relationship between the effectiveness of probation work and the number of offenders is in inverse ratio

46. The fundamental desires for food, shelter, family, and approval, and their accompanying    46.____
instinctive forms of behavior, are among the most important forces in human life because they are essential to and directly connected with the preservation and the welfare of the individual as well as of the race.
According to this statement,

    A. as long as human beings are permitted to act instinctively, they will act wisely
    B. the instinct for self-preservation makes the individual consider his own welfare rather than that of others
    C. racial and individual welfare depend upon the fundamental desires
    D. the preservation of the race demands that instinctive behavior be modified

47. The growth of our cities, the increasing tendency to move from one part of the country to    47.____
another, the existence of people of different cultures in the neighborhood, have together made it more and more difficult to secure group recreation as part of informal family and neighborhood life.
According to this statement,

A. the breaking up of family and neighborhood ties discourages new family and neighborhood group recreation
B. neighborhood recreation no longer forms a significant part of the larger community
C. the growth of cities crowds out the development of all recreational activities
D. the non-English speaking people do not accept new activities easily

48. Sublimation consists in directing some inner urge, arising from a lower psychological level, into some channel of interest on a higher psychological level. Pugnaciousness, for example, is directed into some athletic activity involving combat, such as football or boxing, where rules of fair play and the ethics of the game lift the destructive urge for combat into a constructive experience and offer opportunities for the development of character and personality.
According to this statement,

    A. the manner of self-expression may be directed into constructive activities
    B. athletic activities such as football and boxing are destructive of character
    C. all conscious behavior of high psychological levels indicates the process of sublimation
    D. the rules of fair play are inconsistent with pugnaciousness

49. The interest and curiosity that a child shows in sex matters and activities should be regarded by the probation officer as

    A. a normal interest to be dealt with as one deals with interest in other subjects
    B. something to be disregarded on the assumption that the child will forget about the problem
    C. something to be satisfied by some mythical explanation until the child is old enough to be initiated into the mystery involved
    D. something to be suppressed by threat of punishment

50. When a gang is brought before the court for stealing, the probation officer, in making his pre-probation investigation, should

    A. deal unofficially with the younger ones and officially with the older members of the gang
    B. organize a group of businessmen to take an interest in the members of the gang
    C. recommend that the ringleaders be committed to a child welfare institution and that the others be placed on probation
    D. study each member of the gang and deal with him according to his individual situation

## KEY (CORRECT ANSWERS)

| | | | | |
|---|---|---|---|---|
| 1. D | 11. B | 21. B | 31. A | 41. D |
| 2. C | 12. A | 22. D | 32. A | 42. B |
| 3. C | 13. C | 23. C | 33. B | 43. C |
| 4. A | 14. C | 24. B | 34. D | 44. C |
| 5. D | 15. D | 25. B | 35. C | 45. A |
| 6. B | 16. A | 26. C | 36. D | 46. C |
| 7. C | 17. A | 27. B | 37. D | 47. A |
| 8. D | 18. D | 28. B | 38. B | 48. A |
| 9. B | 19. B | 29. C | 39. D | 49. A |
| 10. A | 20. A | 30. A | 40. B | 50. D |

# TEST 2

DIRECTIONS: Each question or incomplete statement is followed by several suggested answers or completions. Select the one that BEST answers the question or completes the statement. *PRINT THE LETTER OF THE CORRECT ANSWER IN THE SPACE AT THE RIGHT.*

1. The one of the following statements which can MOST conceivably be characterized as true is:

    A. Generally speaking, the younger a person is, the less easily he can be influenced by suggestion.
    B. If a probation officer has sufficient technical knowledge of his duties, it is not necessary for him to exercise tact in dealing with criminal offenders.
    C. A probation officer should reject entirely hearsay evidence in making a social diagnosis of a case.
    D. One of the characteristics of adolescence is a feeling in the child that he is misunderstood.

2. The statement that those parental attitudes are good which offer emotional security to the child BEST expresses the notion that

    A. emotionally secure children do not have feelings of aggression
    B. children should not be held accountable for their actions
    C. parental attitudes are inadequate which do not give the child feelings of belonging and freedom for experience
    D. a family in which there is economic dependence cannot be good for the child

3. When advised of the need for medical treatment over an extended period of time in a locality some distance from home, the parents of a child with a cardiac ailment decide to send him to a home in another town.
   The BEST home for the child in this town would be one

    A. in which there are already residing two foster children who require rest and quiet
    B. in which the family is on relief
    C. in which there are two active boys of the same age as this child
    D. with the bathroom and bedroom on the second floor

4. Rehabilitation of an offender who has presented serious problems can probably be effected BEST by the probation officer who

    A. believes that the behavior is caused by maladjustment and tries to meet the offender's needs accordingly
    B. is kind and just, but punishes the offender for every lapse of good conduct
    C. keeps the offender under constant observation, making him conscious of his behavior deviations
    D. overlooks minor transgressions and rewards the offender for good behavior

5. Making an adjustment upon release under probation or parole, as the case may be, is believed by court workers to be EASIER for the

    A. probationer because the delayed action awaiting his release from probation serves to keep him aware of the necessity of continuing his normal life patterns
    B. parolee because he is able to idealize the security of the penitentiary in his recent experience

C. probationer because he has not been removed from his normal surroundings
D. parolee because frequent visits by family members and close friends during his imprisonment served to provide periodic psychologically uplifting experiences

6. In the granting of probation to a war veteran, the question of leniency on that account should  6.____

    A. not enter because greater leniency to the veteran would give him an unfair advantage over the non-veteran facing the bar with equal guilt
    B. enter because the veteran has made a universally acknowledged contribution to the protection of our society and deserves the protection of his own interests in return
    C. not enter because other important considerations involved in the probation process are the protection of society and the furthering of the best interests of the individual
    D. enter because the military experiences of the veteran may have contributed to his being more irresponsible mentally than the non-veteran

7. During a certain five-year period, it is found that only 66.4 arrests for incest occurred yearly in the city.  7.____
On the basis of this information, the MOST obvious inference for a probation officer to make is that

    A. the research material on which the data are based is definitely incomplete
    B. apprehension for incest can be expected in about 66.4% of the cases in which this crime is committed
    C. very few cases of incest were committed in the city during the stated period
    D. most cases of incest did not become matters of official police information in the city during the stated period

Questions 8-10.

DIRECTIONS:  Questions 8 through 10 are to be answered on the basis of the facts given in the following case history.

Tom Jones - Age 13, I.Q. III

Boy is in 6th grade, school work poor, citizenship fair. He does not constitute a serious behavior problem in school but is often truant.
Relatives

Mother, 33 years of age, divorced father of boy and later remarried. Stepfather and boy did not get along. Stepfather is now out of the home and his whereabouts unknown. Mother is employed in a beauty parlor, earning $255 a week. No other income in family. Woman's mother, age 70, keeps house and looks after boy and his younger sister. Grandmother has absolutely no control over boy.

Sister is 9 years of age, a frail child, never strong, and because of this fact has been *spoiled*.

Boy is undersized, thin, nervous, irritable, and emotional. He likes to read and reads well. Likes WILD WEST and adventure stories. Boy seems fond of his mother. Family lives in a very poor neighborhood.

The mother has an older sister, married, and living on a ranch in Canada. The couple are reported to be fairly well-to-do and have no children. Their ranch is located in a rather remote section. Boy's own father is remarried and living in Seattle. He has two children by his last marriage. Mother is weak and easygoing, passionately fond of both of her children, but inclined to scold them one minute and pet them the next.

Reason Before Court

Boy has been involved with a group of older boys in a series of petty thieveries. Was gone from home for two days at one time and when he returned, told a tale of being kidnapped, which was found later to be entirely imaginary.

8. According to the facts given in the preceding case history, the MOST applicable of the following interpretations for the probation officer to make is

   A. economic factors play a minor part in this case
   B. the boy's taste in reading may indicate a tendency toward instability
   C. removal of the family to a better neighborhood may solve this problem
   D. this is a case for the school authorities to handle because of the truancy involved

9. The conclusion among the following LEAST likely to be reached in a probation report on this case is

   A. the boy's love of adventure and excitement probably contributes to his behavior problem
   B. since the mother lacks stability of character, it would be best to take both children from her
   C. the kidnapping tale, later found to be false, would indicate little possibility of a serious mental defect in the boy
   D. the security of the aunt and uncle's home would be a determining factor in any plan to place the boy with them

10. The one of the following findings LEAST likely to be approved by an experienced probation officer is

    A. the boy can be placed and continued on probation beyond his eighteenth birthday
    B. placement in an *ungraded* class in school might greatly benefit this boy
    C. this family should be referred to a welfare agency in order that the family budget may be supplemented
    D. the greater affection bestowed on the little sister and the consequent jealousy of the boy is probably one of the causes of delinquency

11. The one of the following which is the LEAST valid reason for keeping probation case records is to

    A. maintain an accurate record of the activities of the probationers
    B. meet the legal requirement
    C. provide a record which may be used in appealing from a conviction
    D. provide for continuity of service to the probationer

12. A probation officer is a professional person who has specialized knowledge and skills in the area of casework in an authoritative setting.
    When the period of probation is ended, good probation practice suggests that

    A. the probation officer cease to be interested in the probationer since the case is closed
    B. if there has been a good relationship between officer and probationer, contacts may be continued over a period of years
    C. the probation officer should remain the only person with whom the probationer can feel completely comfortable and confident
    D. the probation officer should maintain continued interest in the probationer so that case files can be built up which may be useful with other probationers

13. The one of the following which, in cases of juvenile delinquency, is NOT an advantage of probation over commitment to an institution is that probation

    A. offers an individualized form of treatment
    B. is less expensive
    C. gives greater protection to the community
    D. leaves the offender in his normal home surroundings

14. In order to alleviate the heavy overcrowding of detention homes, a practice sometimes used in the case of a child awaiting a hearing is his confinement in his own home during the hours when he is not engaged in specific authorized pursuits such as attending school or working.
    The one of the following which is LEAST likely to be a serious problem in home detention is the

    A. inability of probation officers or caseworkers to exercise adequate supervision over the child
    B. deprivation of the child from the companionship of children of his age
    C. possibility that the child's family cannot be depended upon to observe the conditions of detention
    D. continual feeling of shame and embarrassment the child may have when in the company of his siblings or friends

15. Of the following, the CHIEF factor which limits the use of the services of private social casework agencies by probation departments is

    A. the belief by probation departments that the private agencies are unable to give constructive services to the probationers
    B. that the law prohibits use of such services in most types of cases
    C. the reluctance of probationers to accept voluntarily the services of these agencies
    D. the prohibitive cost of these services to the courts

16. Environmental manipulation as an approach to treatment is often required in probation supervision.
Of the following, the BEST illustration of this approach is a case where the probation officer

    A. adopts a positive rather than a negative attitude toward the client's future after his probation is over
    B. suggests physical changes in the probationer's life and makes referrals to various social agencies for assistance
    C. applies his knowledge of casework techniques in every aspect of probation supervision
    D. cautiously makes use of authority in supervision

17. The disparity in the terms of sentences imposed by different judges in criminal courts for identical crimes has been a cause for serious concern.
Of the following, the GREATEST problem involved in the imposition of sentence is that

    A. the judges do not have any basis on which to impose a sentence other than their own judgment
    B. a serious crime may be punishable by a shorter sentence than a minor offense
    C. some judges will enjoy greater popularity than others
    D. the term of sentence a criminal receives is within the limits set for his crime, dependent on varying standards of the judges

18. In penal administration, *indeterminate sentence* means a

    A. sentence the length of which depends upon the behavior and improvement of the convicted person while in prison
    B. long prison sentence at hard labor
    C. sentence with a minimum and a maximum term determined by the judge within statutory limits
    D. sentence based on circumstantial evidence

19. An agency which provides casework help to parent applicants in deciding whether placement of their children is the solution to the family's problem, and in making referrals to community resources if placement is not indicated, is the

    A. Jewish Child Care Association
    B. Little Flower House
    C. Sheltering Arms Children Service
    D. Wiltwyck School

20. An agency providing casework service with psychiatric consultation and psychological testing for girls including unmarried mothers is the

    A. George Junior Republic
    B. Youth Consultation Service
    C. Goddard Neighborhood Center
    D. Girl's Club

21. Jurisdiction over cases involving the protection and treatment of persons under 16 years of age is vested in the _____ Court.

    A. Family     B. Juvenile     C. Supreme     D. County

22. The basic objective of the Judiciary Article of this state is to establish    22._____

    A. unification of all courts in the city, leaving the courts in the rest of the state unchanged in jurisdiction
    B. a unified court system for the entire state with appropriate jurisdictions in each district
    C. a separate court for each category of cases and a separate category of cases for each court
    D. a statewide court for all civil cases and a statewide court for all criminal cases

23. A caseworker in a city agency is planning to refer one of her clients to a private agency in the community.    23._____
    The one of the following which is of GREATEST importance in insuring that the transfer will actually take place is that the

    A. agency is located within the client's proper district
    B. client will cooperate in bringing about such a transfer
    C. caseworker will assure the client that transfer does not mean rejection by the former
    D. agency does not require a fee in excess of what the client can afford

24. The one of the following agencies which provides numerous services to children including recreation, vacation, convalescent care, foster care, and psychiatric service is the    24._____

    A. Child Development Center
    B. Child Welfare League of America
    C. Children's Aid Society
    D. U.S. Children's Bureau

25. Of the following institutions for the chronically ill, the one to which a physically handicapped child would be referred is    25._____

    A. Bird S. Coler Memorial Hospital
    B. Beth Abraham Home
    C. Farm Colony
    D. Josephine Baird Home

26. In planning for the vocational rehabilitation of a physically handicapped person, the use of the sheltered workshop can be a very helpful resource.    26._____
    Of the following, the client for whom such service would be MOST appropriate is the one who

    A. will need a constructive way to spend his time for an indefinite period
    B. because of advanced age, is unable to compete in the labor market
    C. needs a transitional experience between his medical care and undertaking a regular job
    D. has a handicap which permanently precludes any gainful employment

27. A group counseling service to parents focused on the understanding of child development and parent-child relations is available through    27._____

    A. Childville
    B. The Arthur Lehman Counseling Service
    C. The State Association for Mental Health
    D. The Child Study Association of America

28. A patient is being discharged from an institutional setting following an initial diagnosis and stabilizing treatment for a diabetic condition of which he had not been aware. His doctor recommends a diet and medication regime for the patient to follow at home, but the patient is uncertain about his ability to carry this out on his own.
A community resource that might be MOST helpful in such a situation is a

    A. visiting nurse service
    B. homemaker service
    C. neighborhood health center
    D. dietitian's service

29. Experience pragmatically suggests that dislocation from cultural roots and customs makes for tension, insecurity, and anxiety. This holds for the child as well as the adolescent, for the new immigrant as well as the second-generation citizen.
Of the following, the MOST important implication of the above statement is that

    A. anxiety, distress, and incapacity are always personal and can be understood best only through an understanding of the child's present cultural environment
    B. in order to resolve the conflicts caused by the displacement of a child from a home with one cultural background to one with another, it is essential that the child fully replace his old culture with the new one
    C. no treatment goal can be envisaged for a dislocated child which does not involve a value judgment which is itself culturally determined
    D. anxiety and distress result from a child's reaction to culturally oriented treatment goals

30. Accepting the fact that mentally gifted children represent superior heredity, the United States faces an important eugenic problem CHIEFLY because

    A. unless these mentally gifted children mature and reproduce more rapidly than the less intelligent children, the nation is heading for a lowering of the average intelligence of its people
    B. although the mentally gifted child always excels scholastically, he generally has less physical stamina than the normal child and tends to lower the nation's population physically
    C. the mentally subnormal are increasing more rapidly than the mentally gifted in America, thus affecting the overall level of achievement of the gifted child
    D. unless the mental level of the general population is raised to that of the gifted child, the mentally gifted will eventually usurp the reigns of government and dominate the mentally weaker

31. The form of psychiatric treatment which requires the LEAST amount of participation on the part of the patient is

    A. psychoanalysis          B. psychotherapy
    C. shock therapy           D. non-directive therapy

32. Tests administered by psychologists for the PRIMARY purpose of measuring intelligence are known as _____ tests.

    A. projective              B. validating
    C. psychometric            D. apperception

33. In recent years there have been some significant changes in the treatment of patients in state psychiatric hospitals.
These changes are PRIMARILY caused by the use of

    A. electric shock therapy
    B. tranquilizing drugs
    C. steroids
    D. the open ward policy

33.____

34. The psychological test which makes use of a set of 20 pictures, each depicting a dramatic scene is known as the

    A. GOODENOUGH TEST
    B. THEMATIC APPERCEPTION TEST
    C. MINNESOTA MULTIPHASIC PERSONALITY INVENTORY
    D. HEALY PICTURE COMPLETION TEST

34.____

35. One of the MOST effective ways in which experimental psychologists have been able to study the effects on personality of heredity and environment has been through the study of

    A. primitive cultures
    B. identical twins
    C. mental defectives
    D. newborn infants

35.____

36. In hospitals with psychiatric divisions, the psychiatric function is PREDOMINANTLY that of

    A. the training of personnel in all psychiatric disciplines
    B. protection of the community against potentially dangerous psychiatric patients
    C. research and study of psychiatric patients so that new knowledge and information can be made generally available
    D. short-term hospitalization designed to determine diagnosis and recommendations for treatment

36.____

37. Predictions of human behavior on the basis of past behavior frequently are inaccurate because

    A. basic patterns of human behavior are in a continual state of flux
    B. human behavior is not susceptible to explanation of a scientific nature
    C. the underlying psychological mechanisms of behavior are not completely understood
    D. quantitative techniques for the measurement of stimuli and responses are unavailable

37.____

38. Socio-cultural factors are being re-evaluated in casework practice as they influence both the worker and the client in their participation in the casework process.
Of the following factors, the one which is currently being studied MOST widely is the

    A. social class of worker and client and its significance in casework
    B. difference in native intelligence which can be ascribed to racial origin of an individual
    C. cultural values affecting the areas in which an individual functions
    D. necessity in casework treatment of the client's membership in an organized religious group

38.____

39. Deviant behavior is a sociological term used to describe behavior which is not in accord with generally accepted standards. This may include juvenile delinquency, adult criminality, mental or physical illness.
Comparison of normal with deviant behavior is USEFUL because it

    A. makes it possible to establish watertight behavioral descriptions
    B. provides evidence of differential social behavior which distinguishes deviant from normal behavior
    C. indicates that deviant behavior is of no concern to caseworkers
    D. provides no evidence that social role is a determinant of behavior

40. Alcoholism may affect an individual client's ability to function as a spouse, parent, worker, and citizen. Your responsibility to a client with a history of alcoholism is to

    A. interpret to the client the causes of alcoholism as a disease syndrome
    B. work with the alcoholic's family to accept him as he is and to stop trying to reform him
    C. encourage the family of the alcoholic to accept treatment
    D. determine the origins of his particular drinking problem, establish a diagnosis, and work out a treatment plan for him

41. There is a trend to regard narcotic addiction as a form of illness for which the current methods of intervention have not been effective.
Research on the combination of social, psychological, and physical causes of addiction would indicate that social workers should

    A. oppose hospitalization of addicts in institutions
    B. encourage the addict to live normally at home
    C. recognize that there is no successful treatment for addiction and act accordingly
    D. use the existing community facilities differentially for each addict

42. A study of social relationships among delinquent and non-delinquent youth has shown that

    A. delinquent youths generally conceal their true feelings and maintain furtive contacts
    B. delinquents are more impulsive and vivacious than law-abiding boys
    C. non-delinquent youths diminish their active social relationships in order to sublimate any anti-social impulses
    D. delinquent and non-delinquent youths exhibit similar characteristics of impulsiveness and vivaciousness

43. The one of the following which is the CHIEF danger of interpreting the delinquent behavior of a child in terms of morality alone when attempting to get at its causes is that

    A. this tends to overlook the likelihood that the causes of the child's actions are more than a negation of morality and involve varied symptoms of disturbance
    B. a child's moral outlook toward life and society is largely colored by that of his parents, thus encouraging parent-child conflicts
    C. too careful a consideration of the moral aspects of the offense and of the child's needs may often negate the demands of justice in a case
    D. standards of morality may be of no concern to the delinquent and he may not realize the seriousness of his offenses

44. In visiting a school attended by children of a *hard-core* family by your agency, it would generally be ADVISABLE to   44._____

    A. keep the school visit a secret from the family so as not to embarrass the children
    B. encourage the parents to obtain all necessary information themselves
    C. inform the family only if you have secured positive information from the school
    D. have the family fully accept the purpose of the visit beforehand

45. In the process of *reaching out* to service multi-problem families, often many initial appointments are made with adolescents before their parents have received much sustained treatment.
    This practice is   45._____

    A. *undesirable;* adolescents are still subject to parental control and, therefore, the parents should be the focus of treatment
    B. *desirable;* juvenile delinquency is the chief cause of difficulty in multi-problem families
    C. *undesirable;* parental distrust of the worker is increased, thus negating the worker's efforts
    D. *desirable;* adolescents are individual clients and should be so treated

46. A 9-year-old boy is living at home with his remarried, widowed mother, his stepfather, and his 3-year-old half-sister. The boy is being neglected and often severely mistreated by his mother and stepfather. The stepfather resents the boy's presence in the home.
    After failing to correct the situation by discussions with the boy's mother and stepfather, the caseworker should recommend for the boy's welfare   46._____

    A. foster home placement in order to prevent his further mistreatment while corrective educational therapy is used on the parents
    B. permanent separation of the boy from his family as the best means of preventing his continued exposure to the unsatisfactory pressures in the household
    C. placement of the boy outside the household and a stern warning to the parents that similar action will be taken on behalf of the younger child should the situation warrant it
    D. temporary placement of the boy with a foster family until such time as the stepfather is no longer in the household

47. A deserted woman and her 13-year-old son have been receiving public assistance. The woman is drunk most of the time, is known to be consorting with men at all hours, and has been unresponsive to casework treatment. The son has been involved in a few minor incidents which have brought him to the attention of the authorities.
    The BEST action for the caseworker to take at this point in order to keep the son from becoming an outright delinquent is to recommend that   47._____

    A. the mother be arrested and jailed for contributing to the delinquency of a minor and the son be sent to a reformatory
    B. no action be taken against the mother because that will lower her status in the eyes of her son and will further weaken family controls
    C. the son be temporarily placed in a foster home and the mother given treatment for alcoholism
    D. the son be committed to a corrective school where his bad habits can be corrected, since the mother is apparently too sick to assume her responsibilities toward her son

48. A caseworker in a city agency is planning to refer one of her clients to a private agency in the community.
The one of the following which is of GREATEST importance in insuring that the transfer will actually take place is that the

    A. agency is located within the client's proper district
    B. client will cooperate in bringing about such a transfer
    C. caseworker will assure the client that transfer does not mean rejection by the former
    D. agency does not require a fee in excess of what the client can afford

48.___

49. In treating juvenile delinquents, it has been found that there are some who make better social adjustment through group treatment than through an individual casework approach.
In selecting delinquent boys for group treatment, the one of the following which is the MOST important consideration is that

    A. the boys to be treated in one group be friends or from the same community
    B. only boys who consent to group treatment be included in the group
    C. the ages of the boys included in the group vary as much as possible
    D. only boys who have not reacted to an individual casework approach be included in the group

49.___

50. Multi-problem families are generally characterized by various functional indicators.
Of the following, the family which is MOST likely to be a multi-problem family is one which has

    A. unemployed adult family members
    B. parents with diagnosed character disorders
    C. children and parents with a series of difficulties in the community
    D. poor housekeeping standards

50.___

## KEY (CORRECT ANSWERS)

| | | | | |
|---|---|---|---|---|
| 1. D | 11. C | 21. A | 31. C | 41. D |
| 2. C | 12. B | 22. B | 32. C | 42. B |
| 3. A | 13. C | 23. B | 33. B | 43. A |
| 4. A | 14. B | 24. C | 34. B | 44. D |
| 5. C | 15. C | 25. A | 35. B | 45. C |
| 6. C | 16. B | 26. C | 36. D | 46. A |
| 7. D | 17. D | 27. D | 37. C | 47. C |
| 8. C | 18. C | 28. A | 38. C | 48. B |
| 9. B | 19. A | 29. C | 39. B | 49. B |
| 10. A | 20. B | 30. A | 40. D | 50. C |

# EXAMINATION SECTION
## TEST 1

DIRECTIONS: Each question or incomplete statement is followed by several suggested answers or completions. Select the one that BEST answers the question or completes the statement. *PRINT THE LETTER OF THE CORRECT ANSWER IN THE SPACE AT THE RIGHT.*

1. Which of the following provides the BEST rationale for increased government involvement in solving current urban problems?
    A. The cities are not so badly off as they seem to be.
    B. Additional research and experimentation is needed to develop solutions to urban problems.
    C. Our current urban problems have obvious and simple solutions.
    D. The only thing that prevents us from solving urban problems is public opinion.

1.____

2. Ethnic identity as a factor in urban America
    A. has virtually disappeared with the rapid assimilation of second and third generation immigrants
    B. has little influence on patterns of occupational mobility
    C. has become an increasingly important determinant of residential choices
    D. continues to exercise an influence on voting behavior

2.____

3. In recent years, there has been a move to decentralize the governmental structure of some of our largest cities.
The one of the following which provides the WEAKEST argument in favor of decentralization is that decentralization will help to
    A. increase administrative responsiveness to neighborhood needs
    B. promote local democracy by developing local leaders
    C. diminish conflict between communities
    D. develop community cohesion

3.____

4. The decentralization and diffusion of metropolitan areas has resulted in
    A. a dramatic decline in the overall population density of the central city
    B. spatial segregation on the basis of race, ethnicity, and class
    C. slow-down in the rate of suburban growth in comparison to central city growth
    D. benefit to persons from lower socio-economic levels by reducing the population density of the poorest sections of the central city

4.____

5. The concentration of the poor in the core areas of the modern decentralized metropolis can BEST be explained by the
    A. failure of public transport systems to follow the new multi-centered pattern of commercial and industrial dispersion
    B. absence of low-skilled jobs in outlying industrial and commercial sub centers

5.____

C. availability of inexpensive goods and services in the central city
D. need such people feel for the security of familiar surroundings

6. Of the following, the MOST serious shortcoming of urban renewal has been that it has
   A. not attempted to modernize aging downtown areas
   B. curtailed industrial and commercial expansion in the cities
   C. failed to provide adequate housing for poor families forced to move out of their old neighborhoods
   D. not stimulated public support for public housing appropriations

7. The vast majority of blacks who had migrated from the South to northern cities had done so PRIMARILY in order to
   A. join friends and relatives
   B. take specific jobs or look for work
   C. take advantage of superior educational facilities
   D. escape southern racial prejudices

8. The one of the following that is the CHIEF justification for developing area-wide planning in health care is that such planning is likely to
   A. promote effective use of a community's total health resources
   B. minimize the need for consumer participation
   C. reduce the total cost of medical care in a community
   D. reduce the number of physicians needed in a community

9. Of the following, the CHIEF reason that the gridiron design, which consists of straight vertical streets that lie perpendicular to horizontal streets, became the dominant planning motif in urban America is that it
   A. facilitated the movement of automobile traffic to central locations
   B. was a convenient and efficient form of subdividing real estate to maximize its utilization
   C. provided fixed boundaries for neighborhoods
   D. could be easily adapted to topographical variations

10. Which of the following is generally the LARGEST cost factor in acquiring and owning a home?
    A. Building materials
    B. Skilled labor
    C. Interest on mortgage
    D. Builder's profit

11. The federally funded job training programs of the 1960's were INITIALLY conceived on the assumption that
    A. the unemployed lacked the necessary skills to qualify for existing job vacancies
    B. people who dropped out of the labor force lost their motivation to work
    C. public assistance made low wage jobs unattractive to the unemployed
    D. the unemployed would not take menial jobs

12. Which of the following statements about the urban poor is ACCURATE?
    A. The proportion of poor people in central cities is the same as in suburbs.
    B. Persons under the age of eighteen constitute the largest group of poor persons.
    C. The number of poor persons living in households headed by women has declined.
    D. The majority of poor persons are in households headed by men under the age of sixty-five.

13. Which one of the following statements concerning health care in America is CORRECT?
    A. All accepted indices indicate that our general health status is higher than that of other countries.
    B. The quality of our doctors and nurses is higher than in other countries.
    C. All people have equal access to the same quality of such care.
    D. The cost of the same quality of care is lower than in most other countries.

14. Of the following, the MOST serious shortcoming of low income public housing sponsored by the federal government is that
    A. income limitations are imposed upon the tenants
    B. housing administrators place too few restrictions on tenant activities
    C. it competes with the private housing market
    D. it has been built primarily in old and dilapidated neighborhoods

15. Which of the following is the LEAST important factor contributing to the residential segregation of blacks in metropolitan areas?
    A. Violence against the black renter and homeowner in white neighborhoods
    B. Fear by whites that the economic value of their property will decline if blacks move into white neighborhoods
    C. Personal preferences of blacks and whites
    D. Fear by whites that the quality of schools will decline if blacks move into white neighborhoods

16. Which of the following is the MOST regressive form of local taxation? _____ tax.
    A. General sales              B. Property
    C. Personal income            D. Corporate income

17. The property tax has come under attack in metropolitan regions because
    A. it fails to discriminate between different types of property within a single taxing jurisdiction
    B. insufficient revenues are raised by the tax
    C. it fails to tax improvements in property
    D. the same type of property is taxed at different rates in different communities within a region

18. Advocates of the culture of poverty hypothesis maintain that remedial action should center on the
    A. discriminatory practices against minorities
    B. lack of work opportunity
    C. attitudes and behavior of the poor
    D. inequitable distribution of educational facilities

19. The one of the following statements concerning crime in our large cities which is LEAST accurate is that
    A. the readily availability of valuable goods in our affluent society has contributed to the increase in crime
    B. young people have a higher crime rate than adults
    C. the increased ability of poor persons to move about the city has contributed to the increase in crime
    D. murder, rape, and aggravated assault constitute the majority of serious crimes as defined by the F.B.I.'s Uniform Crime Reports

20. In assessing the impact of the automobile and public mass transportation on urban population congestion, it is MOST accurate to state that
    A. the construction of an elaborate metropolitan expressway system will relieve such congestion
    B. neither the automobile nor public mass transportation can relieve such congestion
    C. adequate knowledge about the relationship between such congestion and various modes of transportation is still lacking
    D. both the automobile and public mass transportation promote such congestion

21. The Supreme Court, in March 1973, reversed previous lower court decisions which had tried to establish that the financing of education through local property taxes was unconstitutional.
    These lower court decisions were based on the contention that
    A. the property tax was applied inequitably in certain areas
    B. the property tax is not an important source of local revenues
    C. the quality of a child's education was dependent on the wealth of the community
    D. districts with a small tax base would have to add a *value added tax*

22. The percentage of local revenues which is spent on schools is smaller in urban communities than it is in suburban communities PRIMARILY because
    A. the need for quality education is not as well recognized in urban communities
    B. the tax base of urban communities is insufficient
    C. other public services in urban communities absorb a larger proportion of available funds
    D. commercial enterprises do not pay school taxes

23. The one of the following which BEST describes the trend of the drop-out rate in public high schools during the last five years is that this rate
    A. rose sharply
    B. showed little fluctuation throughout the period and ended at the same level this year as it was five years ago
    C. declined sharply
    D. showed considerable fluctuation throughout the period and ended at the same level this year as it was five years ago

24. One of the findings of the Coleman Report, EQUALITY OF EDUCATIONAL OPPORTUNITY, was that the degree to which black students felt they could affect their environment and future is related to their achievement AND to the
    A. quality of the teaching staff
    B. number of college preparatory courses offered at the high school level
    C. condition of physical facilities
    D. proportion of whites in the school

25. The concept of cultural pluralism is MOST actively opposed by
    A. the Amish
    B. supporters of black studies as a discipline
    C. supporters of bilingual education
    D. supporters of parochial schools

## KEY (CORRECT ANSWERS)

| | | | |
|---|---|---|---|
| 1. | B | 11. | A |
| 2. | D | 12. | B |
| 3. | C | 13. | B |
| 4. | D | 14. | D |
| 5. | A | 15. | A |
| 6. | C | 16. | A |
| 7. | B | 17. | D |
| 8. | A | 18. | C |
| 9. | B | 19. | D |
| 10. | C | 20. | C |

| | |
|---|---|
| 21. | C |
| 22. | C |
| 23. | A |
| 24. | D |
| 25. | A |

# TEST 2

DIRECTIONS: Each question or incomplete statement is followed by several suggested answers or completions. Select the one that BEST answers the question or completes the statement. *PRINT THE LETTER OF THE CORRECT ANSWER IN THE SPACE AT THE RIGHT.*

1. When police provide patrol services on the basis of workload, a high concentration of patrol officers in minority group neighborhoods often results. The police then are subject to criticism both from minority residents who feel persecuted by the police and from residents of other neighborhoods who feel they are not receiving the same level of police protection.
Which one of the following BEST states both whether or not, under these conditions, patrol distribution should be changed and also the BEST reason therefor?
It should
    A. *not be changed*, because community pressure should not be allowed to influence police decisions
    B. *be changed*, because all neighborhoods in the community are entitled to the same level of police protection
    C. *be changed*, because it is necessary for the police to respond to community pressures in order to improve community relations
    D. *not be changed*, because having police concentration in minority neighborhoods protects the remainder of the community from riot situations
    E. *not be changed*, because to do so would deprive law-abiding minority neighborhood residents of police protection to their need

1.____

2. A certain boy is raised by parents who are concerned with status, social position the *right* occupation, the *right* friends, the *right* neighborhood, etc. Social behavior plays a vital role in their lives, and their outlook with regard to rearing children can best be summed up by *children should be seen and not heard*. Following are four descriptive terms their son might possibly be likely to use if he were asked to describe the *perfect boy*:
    I.  Being polite
    II. Being a good companion
    III. Being clean
    IV. Being fun
Which one of the following choices MOST accurately classifies the above statements into those the boy is MOST likely to use when describing the *perfect boy* and those which he is LEAST likely to use?
He is
    A. most likely to use I and II and least likely to use III and IV
    B. most likely to use I and III and least likely to use II and IV
    C. most likely to use I, II, and III and least likely to use IV
    D. most likely to use II and IV and least likely to use I and III
    E. equally likely to use any of I, II, III, and IV

2.____

3. People adjust to frustrations or conflicts in many different words.  One of these ways of adjustment is known as projection.
Which one of the following behaviors is the BEST example of projection?
A person
   A. who is properly arrested for inciting a riot protests against police brutality and violence
   B. stopped for going through a red light claims that he couldn't help it because his brakes wouldn't hold
   C. who is arrested for a crime persistently claims to have forgotten the whole incident that led to his arrest
   D. who is arrested for a crime cries, screams, and stamps his feet on the floor like a child having a temper tantrum
   E. who is stopped for a traffic violation claims that he is a close friend of the mayor in order to escape blame for the violation

3.____

4. A certain police officer was patrolling a playground area where adolescent gangs had been causing troubles and holding drinking parties.  He approached a teenage boy who was alone and drinking from a large paper cup.  He asked the boy what he was drinking, and the boy replied *Coke*.  The officer asked the boy for the cup, and the boy refused to give it to him.  The officer then explained that he wanted to check the contents, and the boy still refused to give it to him.  The officer then demanded the cup, and the boy reluctantly gave it to him.  The officer smelled the contents of the cup and determined that it was, in fact, Coke.  He then told the boy to move along and emptied the Coke on the ground.
Which one of the following is the MOST serious error, if any, made by the officer in handling this situation?
   A. The officer should not have made any effort to determine what was in the cup.
   B. The officer should not have explained to the boy why he wanted to have the cup.
   C. The officer should have returned the Coke to the boy and allowed the boy to stay where he was.
   D. The officer should have first placed the boy under arrest before taking the cup from him.
   E. None of the above since the officer made no error in handling the situation.

4.____

5. Sociological studies have revealed a great deal of information about the behavior and characteristics of homosexuals.
Which one of the following statements about male homosexuals is MOST accurate?
   A. Male homosexual activity is engaged in by less than 10% of the population.
   B. Most male homosexuals would like to be cured if it were possible.
   C. Male homosexuals are more likely than other sex deviates to commit assaults on female children.
   D. Most male homosexuals pose a threat to the morals and safety of a community and should be removed from the streets.

5.____

E. Most male homosexuals pose no threat to a community and are content to restrict their activities to people of similar tastes.

6. Which one of the following is the MOST important factor for the police department to consider in building a good public image?
    A. A good working relationship with the news media
    B. An efficient police-community relations program
    C. An efficient system for handling citizen complaints
    D. The proper maintenance of police facilities and equipment
    E. The behavior of individual officers in their contacts with the public

6._____

7. Following are four aspects of Black culture which sociologists and psychologists might possibly consider as health aspects:
    I. Use of hair straighteners    II. Use of skin bleaches
    III. Use of natural Afro hair styles    IV. Use of African style of dress
    Which one of the following MOST accurately classifies the above into those that sociologists do consider healthy and those that they do not?
    A. I and III are considered healthy, but II and IV are not
    B. I, III, and IV are considered healthy but II is not
    C. None of I, II, III, and IV is considered healthy
    D. III is considered healthy, but I, II, and IV are not
    E. III and IV are considered healthy, but I and II are not

7._____

8. Which one of the following situations is MOST responsible for making police-community relations more difficult in a densely populated, low income precinct?
    A. The majority of residents in such precincts do not want police on patrol in their communities.
    B. Radio patrol car sectors in such precincts are too small to give patrol officers an understanding of community problems
    C. The higher ratio of arrests per capita in such precincts leads law-abiding residents in such a precinct to feel oppressed by police.
    D. Such precincts tend to have little or no communication among residents so efforts to improve police-community relations must be on an individual level.
    E. This type of precinct has a higher rate of crime and, therefore, law-abiding residents are often bitter because they feel the police give them inferior protection.

8._____

9. Research studies based on having children draw pictures of police officers at work have shown that children of low income minority group parents are more likely to see police as aggressive than children of upper-middle class white parents. One police department had a group of low-income children participate in a 20-minute discussion with a police officer, and then allowed the youngsters a chance to sit in a police car, blow the siren, etc.
Which one of the following BEST states what effect, if any, this approach MOST likely had on the pictures drawn by the children when they were released two days later?
    A. The children showed almost no hostility toward police.
    B. The children showed significantly less hostility toward police.

9._____

C. The children showed significantly more hostility toward police.
D. There was essentially no change in the attitudes of the children.
E. The children showed a loss of respect for the police, who saw them as weak and permissive

10. Following are three possible complaints against police which might be made frequently by blacks living in cities where riots have taken place:
    I. Lack of adequate channels for complaints against police officers
    II. Failure of police departments to provide adequate protection for Blacks
    III. Discriminatory police employment or promotional practices with regard to Black officers
    Which one of the following choices MOST accurately classifies the above into those which have been frequent complaints and those which have not?
    A. I is a frequent complaint, but II and III are not.
    B. I and II are frequent complaints, but III is not.
    C. I and III are frequent complaints, but II is not.
    D. All of I, II, and III are frequent complaints.
    E. None of I, II, or III is a frequent complaint.

11. A career criminal is one who actively engages in crime as his lifework. Which one of the following statements about *career criminals* is MOST accurate?
    A *career criminal*
    A. understands that prison is a normal occupational hazard
    B. is very likely to suffer from deep emotional and psychological problems
    C. has a lower average intelligence than the average for the general public
    D. is just as likely to engage in violence during a crime as any other criminal
    E. is less likely to have begun his crime career as a juvenile when compared to other criminals

12. Which one of the following choices BEST describes the tactic of non-violent resistance as used by civil rights groups?
    The
    A. willingness of persons to accept unlawful arrest without resistance
    B. avoiding of prosecution for violations of law by refusing to appear in court when required
    C. teasing and verbal harassment of police officers in order to cause unlawful arrests
    D. intentional violation of a particular law by persons unwilling to accept the penalty for violating that law
    E. intentional violation of a particular law by persons willing to accept the penalty for violating that law

13. Which one of the following is the MOST accurate statement about the civil disorders that occurred in the United States in the first nine months of 1967?
    A. Damage caused by riots was much greater than initial estimates indicated.
    B. They intended to be unplanned outbursts, not events planned by militants or agitators.

C. The principal targets of attack were homes, schools, and businesses owned by Black merchants.
D. There were very few minor riots; either there were major riots or there were no riots.
E. The majority of persons killed or injured in the disorders were police officers and white civilians.

14. Some managers try to achieve goals by manipulating or deceiving subordinates into doing what the managers want. Such a manager normally is motivated by a desire to control people or by a desire to hide his own inadequacies. Such a manager also wants to hide the reasons for his actions from those he manages. This type of manager is often referred to as a *facade builder*. Which one of the following types of behavior is LEAST characteristic of this type of manager.
He
    A. shows concern for other people
    B. avoids criticizing other people
    C. gives praise and approval easily
    D. delegates responsibility for administering punishment
    E. avoids getting involved in internal conflicts within the organization

14.____

15. Which one of the following choices states both the MOST PROBABLE effect on crime rate statistics of increased public confidence in police and also the MOST IMPORTANT reason for this effect?
    A. The overall statistical crime rate would decrease because people would be less likely to commit crimes.
    B. The overall statistical crime rate would increase because people would be more likely to report crimes.
    C. The overall statistical crime rate would increase because police would probably be clearing more crimes by arrest.
    D. The overall statistical crime rate would decrease because police would be less likely to arrest offender for minor violations.
    E. Increased public confidence in police would have no effect on the overall statistical crime rate because this depends on the number of crimes committed, not public attitude toward police.

15.____

16. One of the important tasks of any administrator is the development of a proper filing system for classifying written documents by subject.
Following are three suggested rules for subject cross-referencing which might possibly be considered proper:
    I. All filed material should have at least one subject cross-reference.
    II. There should be no limit on the number of subject cross-references that may be made for a single record.
    III. The original document should be filed under the primary classification subject, with only cross-reference sheets, not considered as records, being filed under the cross-reference subject classifications.

16.____

Which one of the following choices MOST accurately classifies the above into those that are proper rules for cross-referencing and those that are not?
- A. I is a proper rule, but II and III are not.
- B. I and III are proper rules, but II is not.
- C. II and III are proper rules, but I is not
- D. III is a proper rule, but I and II are not.
- E. None of I, II, and III is a proper rule.

17. Wherever gambling, prostitution, and narcotics distribution openly flourish, they are usually accompanied by community charges of *protection* on the part of local police.
Which one of the following BEST states both whether or not such changes have merit and also the BEST reason therefor?
The charges
- A. *do not have, merit* because the nature of these operations makes them very difficult to detect
- B. *have merit*, because such operations cannot long continue openly without some measure of police protection
- C. *have merit*, because offenses of this type are among the easiest to eliminate
- D. *do not have merit*, because the local patrol forces probably do not have responsibility for large-scale vice enforcement
- E. *do not have merit*, because vice flourishes openly only in a community which desires it; therefore, it is the community that is providing the protection

18. The PRIMARY function of a department of social services is to
- A. refer needy persons to legally responsible relatives for support
- B. enable needy persons to become self-supporting
- C. refer ineligible persons to private agencies
- D. grant aid to needy eligible persons
- E. administer public assistance programs in which the federal and state governments do not participate

19. A public assistance program objective should be designed to
- A. provide for eligible persons in accordance with their individual requirements and with consideration of the circumstances in which they live
- B. provide for eligible persons at a standard of living equal to that enjoyed while they were self-supporting
- C. make sure that assistance payments from public funds are not too liberal
- D. guard against providing a better living for persons receiving aid than is enjoyed by the most frugal independent families
- E. eliminate the need for private welfare agencies

20. It is often stated that it would be better to abolish the need for relief rather than to extend the existing public assistance programs.

This statement suggests that
- A. existing legislation makes it too easy for people to apply for and receive assistance
- B. public assistance should be limited to institutional care for rehabilitative purposes
- C. the support of needy persons should be the responsibility of their own families and relatives rather than that of the government
- D. the existing criteria used to determine *need* for public assistance are too liberal and should be modified to include a *work test*
- E. attempts should be made to eradicate those forces in our social organization which cause poverty

21. The one of the following types of public assistance which is FREQUENTLY described as a *special privilege* is
    - A. veteran assistance
    - B. emergency assistance
    - C. aid to dependent children
    - D. old-age assistance
    - E. vocational rehabilitation of the handicapped

22. The principle of *settlement* holds that each community is responsible for the care of its own members and that communities should not bear the costs of care for needy non-residents.
    This was an intrinsic principle of the
    - A. English Poor Laws
    - B. Home Rule Amendment
    - C. Single Tax Proposal
    - D. National Bankruptcy Regulations
    - E. Proportional Representation Act

23. The FIRST form of state social security legislation developed in the United States was
    - A. health insurance
    - B. unemployment compensation
    - C. workmen's compensation
    - D. old-age insurance
    - E. old-age assistance

24. The plan for establishing a federal government with Cabinet formerly called the Department of Health, Education, and Welfare was
    - A. vetoed by the President after having been passed by Congress
    - B. disapproved by the Senate after having been passed by the House of Representatives
    - C. rejected by both the Senate and the House of Representatives
    - D. enacted into legislation
    - E. determined to be unconstitutional

25. Census Bureau reports show certain definite social trends in our population. One of these trends which was a MAJOR contributing factor in the establishment of the federal old-age insurance system is the
    - A. increased rate of immigration to the United States
    - B. rate at which the number of Americans living to 65 years of age and beyond is increasing

C. increasing amounts spent for categorical relief in the country as a whole
D. decreasing number of legally responsible relatives who have been unable to assist he aged since the depression of 1929
E. number of states which have failed to meet their obligations in the care of the aged

---

## KEY (CORRECT ANSWERS)

| | | | |
|---|---|---|---|
| 1. | E | 11. | A |
| 2. | B | 12. | E |
| 3. | A | 13. | B |
| 4. | C | 14. | E |
| 5. | E | 15. | B |
| 6. | E | 16. | C |
| 7. | E | 17. | B |
| 8. | E | 18. | D |
| 9. | B | 19. | A |
| 10. | D | 20. | E |
| 21. | A | | |
| 22. | A | | |
| 23. | C | | |
| 24. | D | | |
| 25. | B | | |

---

# EXAMINATION SECTION
## TEST 1

DIRECTIONS: Each question or incomplete statement is followed by several suggested answers or completions. Select the one that BEST answers the question or completes the statement. *PRINT THE LETTER OF IN THE CORRECT ANSWER THE SPACE AT THE RIGHT.*

1. Reports show that more men than women are physically handicapped MAINLY because          1.____

   A. women are instinctively more cautious than men
   B. men are more likely to have congenital deformities
   C. women tend to seek surgical remedies because of greater concern over personal appearance
   D. men have lower ability to recover from injury
   E. men are more likely to be exposed to hazardous conditions

2. Of the following, the explanation married women give MOST frequently for seeking employment outside the home is that they wish to          2.____

   A. escape the drudgeries of home life
   B. develop secondary employment skills
   C. maintain an emotionally satisfying career
   D. provide the main support for the family
   E. supplement the family income

3. Of the following home conditions, the one *most likely* to cause emotional disturbances in children is          3.____

   A. increased birthrate following the war
   B. disrupted family relationships
   C. lower family income than that of neighbors
   D. higher family income than that of neighbors
   E. overcrowded living conditions

4. Casual unemployment, as distinguished from other types of unemployment, is traceable MOST readily to          4.____

   A. a decrease in the demand for labor as a result of scientific progress
   B. more or less haphazard changes in the demand for labor in certain industries
   C. periodic changes in the demand for labor in certain industries
   D. disturbances and disruptions in industry resulting from international trade barriers
   E. increased mobility of the population

5. Labor legislation, although primarily intended for the benefit of the employee, MAY aid the employer by          5.____

   A. increasing his control over the immediate labor market
   B. prohibiting government interference with operating policies
   C. protecting him, through equalization of labor costs, from being undercut by other employers
   D. transferring to the general taxpayer the principal costs of industrial hazards of accident and unemployment
   E. increasing the pensions of civil service employees

6. When employment and unemployment figures both decline, the MOST probable conclusion is that

   A. the population has reached a condition of equilibrium
   B. seasonal employment has ended
   C. the labor force has decreased
   D. payments for unemployment insurance have been increased
   E. industrial progress has reduced working hours

7. An individual with an I.Q. of 100 may be said to have demonstrated _____ intelligence.

   A. superior
   B. absolute
   C. substandard
   D. approximately average
   E. high average

8. While state legislatures differ in many respects, all of them are *most nearly* alike in

   A. provisions for retirement of members
   B. rate of pay
   C. length of legislative sessions
   D. method of selection of their members
   E. length of term of office

9. If a state passed a law in a field under Congressional jurisdiction and if Congress subsequently passed contrary legislation, the state provision would be

   A. regarded as never having existed
   B. valid until the next session of the state legislature, which would be obliged to repeal it
   C. superseded by the federal statute
   D. ratified by Congress
   E. still operative in the state involved

10. Power to pardon offenses committed against the people of the United States is vested in the

    A. Supreme Court of the United States
    B. United States District Courts
    C. Federal Bureau of Investigation
    D. United States Parole Board
    E. President of the United States

11. As distinguished from formal social control of an individual's behavior, an example of informal social control is that exerted by

    A. public opinion
    B. religious doctrine
    C. educational institutions
    D. statutes
    E. public health measures

12. The PRINCIPAL function of the jury in a jury trial is to decide questions of

    A. equity
    B. fact
    C. injunction
    D. contract
    E. law

13. Of the following rights of an individual, the one which usually depends on citizenship as distinguished from those given anyone living under the laws of the United States is the right to  13.____

    A. receive public assistance
    B. hold an elective office
    C. petition the government for redress of grievances
    D. receive equal protection of the laws
    E. be accorded a trial by jury

14. If the characteristics of a person were being studied by competent observers, it would be expected that their observations would differ MOST markedly with respect to their evaluation of the person's  14.____

    A. intelligence
    B. nutritional condition
    C. temperamental characteristics
    D. weight
    E. height

15. If there are evidences of dietary deficiency in families where cereals make up a major portion of the diet, the *most likely* reason for this deficiency is that  15.____

    A. cereals cause absorption of excessive quantities of water
    B. persons who concentrate their diet on cereals do not chew their food properly
    C. carbohydrates are deleterious
    D. other essential food elements are omitted
    E. children eat cereals too rapidly

16. Although malnutrition is generally associated with poverty, dietary studies of population groups in the United States reveal that  16.____

    A. malnutrition is most often due to a deficiency of nutrients found chiefly in high-cost foods
    B. there has been overemphasis of the casual relationship between poverty and malnutrition
    C. malnutrition is found among people with sufficient money to be well fed
    D. a majority of the population in all income groups is undernourished
    E. malnutrition is not a factor in the incidence of rickets

17. The organization which has as one of its primary functions the mitigation of suffering caused by famine, fire, floods, and other national calamities is the  17.____

    A. National Safety Council
    B. Salvation Army
    C. Public Administration Service
    D. American National Red Cross
    E. American Legion

18. The MAIN difference between public welfare and private social agencies is that in public agencies,

    A. case records are open to the public
    B. the granting of assistance cannot be sufficiently flexible to meet the varying needs of individual recipients
    C. only financial assistance may be provided
    D. all policies and procedures must be based upon statutory authorizations
    E. economical and efficient administration are stressed because their funds are obtained through public taxation

19. A recipient of relief who is in need of the services of an attorney but is unable to pay the customary fees, should *generally* be referred to the

    A. Small Claims Court
    B. Domestic Relations Court
    C. County Lawyers Association
    D. City Law Department
    E. Legal Aid Society

20. An injured workman should file his claim for workmen's compensation with the

    A. State Labor Relations Board
    B. Division of Placement and Unemployment Insurance
    C. State Industrial Commission
    D. Workmen's Compensation Board
    E. State Insurance Board

21. The type of insurance found MOST frequently among families such as those assisted by the Department of Social Services is

    A. accident
    B. straight life
    C. endowment
    D. industrial
    E. personal liability

22. Of the following items in the standard budget of the Department of Social Services, the one for which actual expenditures would be MOST constant throughout the year is

    A. fuel
    B. housing
    C. medical care
    D. clothing
    E. household replacements

23. The MOST frequent cause of "broken homes" is attributed to the

    A. temperamental incompatibilities of parents and in-laws
    B. extension of the system of children's courts
    C. psychopathic irresponsibility of the parents
    D. institutionalization of one of the spouses
    E. death of one or both spouses

24. In rearing children, the problems of the widower are usually greater than those of the widow, largely because of the

    A. tendency of widowers to impose excessively rigid moral standards
    B. increased economic hardship
    C. added difficulty of maintaining a desirable home
    D. possibility that a stepmother will be added to the household
    E. prevalent masculine prejudice against pursuits which are inherently feminine

25. Foster-home placement of children is often advocated in preference to institutionalization *primarily* because

    A. the law does not provide for local supervision of children's institutions
    B. institutions furnish a more expensive type of care
    C. the number of institutions is insufficient compared to the number of children needing care
    D. children are not well treated in institutions
    E. foster homes provide a more normal environment for children

## KEY (CORRECT ANSWERS)

| | | | |
|---|---|---|---|
| 1. | E | 11. | A |
| 2. | E | 12. | B |
| 3. | B | 13. | B |
| 4. | B | 14. | C |
| 5. | C | 15. | D |
| 6. | C | 16. | C |
| 7. | D | 17. | D |
| 8. | D | 18. | D |
| 9. | C | 19. | E |
| 10. | E | 20. | D |

21. D
22. B
23. E
24. C
25. E

# TEST 2

DIRECTIONS: Each question or incomplete statement is followed by several suggested answers or completions. Select the one that BEST answers the question or completes the statement. *PRINT THE LETTER OF THE CORRECT ANSWER IN THE SPACE AT THE RIGHT.*

1. Of the following, the category MOST likely to yield the greatest reduction in cost to the taxpayer under improved employment conditions is  1.___

    A. home relief, including aid to the homeless
    B. aid to the blind
    C. aid to dependent children
    D. old-age assistance

2. One of the MOST common characteristics of the chronic alcoholic is  2.___

    A. low intelligence level     B. wanderlust
    C. psychosis                  D. egocentricity

3. Of the following factors leading toward the cure of the alcoholic, the MOST important is thought to be  3.___

    A. removal of all alcohol from the immediate environment
    B. development of a sense of personal adequacy
    C. social disapproval of drinking
    D. segregation from former companions

4. The Federal Housing Administration is the agency which  4.___

    A. insures mortgages made by lending institutions for new construction or remodeling of old construction
    B. provides federal aid for state and local government for slum clearance and housing for very low income families
    C. subsidizes the building industry through direct grants
    D. provides for the construction of low-cost housing projects owned and operated by the federal government

5. In comparing the advantages of foster home over institutional placement, it is generally agreed that institutional care is LEAST advisable for children  5.___

    A. who cannot sustain the intimacy of foster family living because of their experiences with their own parents
    B. who are socially well-adjusted or have had considerable experience in living with a family
    C. who have need for special facilities for observation, diagnosis, and treatment
    D. whose natural parents find it difficult to accept the idea of foster home placement because of its close resemblance to adoption

6. The school can play a vital part in detecting the child who displays overt symptomatic behavior indicative of social maladjustment CHIEFLY because the teacher has the opportunity to

   A. assume a pseudo-parental role in regard to discipline and punishment, thereby limiting the extent of the maladjusted child's anti-social behavior
   B. observe how the child relates to the group and what reactions are stimulated in him by his peer relationships
   C. determine whether the adjustment difficulties displayed by the child were brought on by the teacher herself or by the other students
   D. help the child's parents to resolve the difficulties in adjustment which are indicated by the child's reactions to the social pressures exerted by his peers

7. In treating juvenile delinquents, it has been found that there are some who make better social adjustment through group treatment than through an individual casework approach.
   In selecting delinquent boys for group treatment, the one of the following which is the MOST important consideration is that

   A. the boys to be treated in one group be friends or from the same community
   B. only boys who consent to group treatment be included in the group
   C. the ages of the boys included in the group vary as much as possible
   D. only boys who have not reacted to an individual casework approach be included in the group

8. Multi-problem families are generally characterized by various functional indicators.
   Of the following, the family which is *most likely* to be a multi-problem family is one which has

   A. unemployed adult family members
   B. parents with diagnosed character disorders
   C. children and parents with a series of difficulties in the community
   D. poor housekeeping standards

9. Multi-problem families generally have a complex history of intervention by a variety of social agencies.
   Of the following phases involved in planning for their treatment, the one which is MOST important to consider FIRST is the

   A. joint decision to limit any help to be given
   B. analysis of facts and definition of the problems involved
   C. determination of treatment priorities
   D. study of available community resources

10. The development of good public relations in the area for which the supervisor is responsible should be considered by the supervisor as

    A. not his responsibility as he is primarily responsible for his workers' services
    B. dependent upon him as he is in the best position to interpret the department to the community
    C. not important to the adequate functioning of the department
    D. a part of his method of carrying out his job responsibility as what his workers do affects the community

11. Of the following, the LEAST accurate statement concerning the relationship of public and private social agencies is that

    A. both have an important and necessary function to perform
    B. they are not to be considered as competing or rival agencies
    C. they are cooperating agencies
    D. their work is based on fundamentally different social work concepts

12. Of the following, the LEAST accurate statement concerning the worker-client relationship is that the worker should have the ability to

    A. express warmth of feeling in appropriate ways as a basis for a professional relationship which creates confidence
    B. feel appropriately in the relationship without losing the ability to see the situation in the perspective necessary to help the people immersed in it
    C. identify himself with the client so that the worker's personality does not influence the client
    D. use keen observation and perceive what is significant with a new range of appreciation of the meaning of the situation to the client

13. Of the following, the MOST fundamental psychological concept underlying case work in the public assistance field is that

    A. eligibility for public assistance should be reviewed from time to time
    B. workers should be aware of the prevalence of psychological disabilities among members of families on public assistance
    C. workers should realize the necessity of carrying out the policies laid down by the state office in order that state aid may be received
    D. in the process of receiving assistance, recipients should not be deprived of their normal status of self-direction

14. Of the following, the MOST comprehensive as well as the MOST accurate statement concerning the professional attitude of the social worker is that he should

    A. have a real concern for, and an intelligent interest in, the welfare of the client
    B. recognize that the client's feelings rather than the realities of his needs are of major importance to the client
    C. put at the client's service the worker's knowledge and sincere interest in him
    D. use his insight and understanding to make sound decisions about the client

15. The one of the following reasons for refusing a job which is LEAST acceptable, from the viewpoint of maintaining a client's continued rights to unemployment insurance benefits, is that

    A. acceptance of the job would interfere with the client's joining or retaining membership in a labor union
    B. there is a strike, lockout, or other industrial controversy in the establishment where employment is offered
    C. the distance from the place of employment to his home is greater than seems justified to the client
    D. the wages offered are lower than the prevailing wages in that locality

16. Experience pragmatically suggests that dislocation from cultural roots and customs makes for tension, insecurity, and anxiety. This holds for the child as well as the adolescent, for the new immigrant as well as the second-generation citizen.
    Of the following, the MOST important implication of the above statement for a social worker in any setting is that

    A. anxiety, distress, and incapacity are always personal and can be understood best only through an understanding of the child's present cultural environment
    B. in order to resolve the conflicts caused by the displacement of a child from a home with one cultural background to one with another, it is essential that the child fully replace his old culture with the new one
    C. no treatment goal can be envisaged for a dislocated child which does not involve a value judgment which is itself culturally determined
    D. anxiety and distress result from a child's reaction to culturally oriented treatment goals

17. Accepting the fact that mentally gifted children represent superior heredity, the United States faces an important eugenic problem CHIEFLY because

    A. unless these mentally gifted children mature and reproduce more rapidly than the less intelligent children, the nation is heading for a lowering of the average intelligence of its people
    B. although the mentally gifted child always excels scholastically, he generally has less physical stamina than the normal child and tends to lower the nation's population physically
    C. the mentally subnormal are increasing more rapidly than the mentally gifted in America, thus affecting the overall level of achievement of the gifted child
    D. unless the mental level of the general population is raised to that of the gifted child, the mentally gifted will eventually usurp the reigns of government and dominate the mentally weaker

18. The form of psychiatric treatment which requires the LEAST amount of participation on the part of the patient is

    A. psychoanalysis            B. psychotherapy
    C. shock therapy             D. non-directive therapy

19. Tests administered by psychologists for the PRIMARY purpose of measuring intelligence are known as _____ tests.

    A. projective
    B. validating
    C. psychometric
    D. apperception

20. In recent years, there have been some significant changes in the treatment of patients in state psychiatric hospitals. These changes are PRIMARILY caused by the use of

    A. electric shock therapy
    B. tranquilizing drugs
    C. steroids
    D. the open-ward policy

21. The psychological test which makes use of a set of twenty pictures, each depicting a dramatic scene, is known as the

    A. Goodenough Test
    B. Thematic Apperception Test
    C. Minnesota Multiphasic Personality Inventory
    D. Healy Picture Completion Test

22. One of the MOST effective ways in which experimental psychologists have been able to study the effects on personality of heredity and environment has been through the study of

    A. primitive cultures
    B. identical twins
    C. mental defectives
    D. newborn infants

23. In hospitals with psychiatric divisions, the psychiatric function is PREDOMINANTLY that of

    A. the training of personnel in all psychiatric disciplines
    B. protection of the community against potentially dangerous psychiatric patients
    C. research and study of psychiatric patients so that new knowledge and information can be made generally available
    D. short-term hospitalization designed to determine diagnosis and recommendations for treatment

24. Predictions of human behavior on the basis of past behavior frequently are INACCURATE because

    A. basic patterns of human behavior are in a continual state of flux
    B. human behavior is not susceptible to explanation of a scientific nature
    C. the underlying psychological mechanisms of behavior are not completely understood
    D. quantitative techniques for the measurement of stimuli and responses are unavailable

25. Socio-cultural factors are being re-evaluated in casework practice as they influence both the worker and the client in their participation in the casework process.
Of the following factors, the one which is currently being studied MOST widely is the

    A. social class of worker and client and its significance in casework
    B. difference in native intelligence which can be ascribed to racial origin of an individual
    C. cultural values affecting the areas in which an individual functions
    D. necessity in casework treatment of the client's membership in an organized religious group

25.____

# KEY (CORRECT ANSWERS)

| 1. A | 11. D |
|------|-------|
| 2. D | 12. C |
| 3. B | 13. D |
| 4. A | 14. C |
| 5. B | 15. C |
| 6. B | 16. C |
| 7. B | 17. A |
| 8. C | 18. C |
| 9. B | 19. C |
| 10. D | 20. B |

21. B
22. B
23. D
24. C
25. C

# EXAMINATION SECTION
## TEST 1

DIRECTIONS: Each question or incomplete statement is followed by several suggested answers or completions. Select the one that BEST answers the question or completes the statement. *PRINT THE LETTER OF THE CORRECT ANSWER IN THE SPACE AT THE RIGHT.*

1. Deviant behavior is a sociological term used to describe behavior which is not in accord with generally accepted standards. This may include juvenile delinquency, adult criminality, mental or physical illness.
 Comparison of normal with deviant behavior is useful to social workers because it

    A. makes it possible to establish watertight behavioral descriptions
    B. provides evidence of differential social behavior which distinguishes deviant from normal behavior
    C. indicates that deviant behavior is of no concern to social workers
    D. provides no evidence that social role is a determinant of behavior

    1.____

2. Alcoholism may affect an individual client's ability to function as a spouse, parent, worker, and citizen.
 A social worker's MAIN responsibility to a client with a history of alcoholism is to

    A. interpret to the client the causes of alcoholism as a disease syndrome
    B. work with the alcoholic's family to accept him as he is and stop trying to reform him
    C. encourage the family of the alcoholic to accept casework treatment
    D. determine the origins of his particular drinking problem, establish a diagnosis, and work out a treatment plan for him

    2.____

3. There is a trend to regard narcotic addiction as a form of illness for which the current methods of intervention have not been effective.
 Research on the combination of social, psychological, and physical causes of addiction would indicate that social workers should

    A. oppose hospitalization of addicts in institutions
    B. encourage the addict to live normally at home
    C. recognize that there is no successful treatment for addiction and act accordingly
    D. use the existing community facilities differentially for each addict

    3.____

4. A study of social relationships among delinquent and non-delinquent youth has shown that

    A. delinquent youth generally conceal their true feelings and maintain furtive social contacts
    B. delinquents are more impulsive and vivacious than law-abiding boys
    C. non-delinquent youths diminish their active social relationships in order to sublimate any anti-social impulses
    D. delinquent and non-delinquent youths exhibit similar characteristics of impulsiveness and vivaciousness

    4.____

5. The one of the following which is the CHIEF danger of interpreting the delinquent behavior of a child in terms of morality *alone* when attempting to get at its causes is that

    A. this tends to overlook the likelihood that the causes of the child's actions are more than a negation of morality and involve varied symptoms of disturbance
    B. a child's moral outlook toward life and society is largely colored by that of his parents, thus encouraging parent-child conflict
    C. too careful a consideration of the moral aspects of the offense and of the child's needs may often negate the demands of justice in a case
    D. standards of morality may be of no concern to the delinquent and he may not realize the seriousness of his offenses

5.\_\_\_

6. Experts in the field of personnel administration are generally agreed that an employee should not be under the immediate supervision of more than one supervisor. A certain worker, because of an emergency situation, divides his time equally between two limited caseloads on a prearranged time schedule. Each unit has a different supervisor, and the worker performs substantially the same duties in each caseload.
The above statement is pertinent in this situation CHIEFLY because

    A. each supervisor, feeling that the cases in her unit should have priority, may demand too much of the worker's time
    B. the two supervisors may have different standards of work performance and may prefer different methods of doing the work
    C. the worker works part-time on each caseload and may not have full knowledge or control of the situation in either caseload
    D. the task of evaluating the worker's services will be doubled, with two supervisors instead of one having to rate his work

6.\_\_\_

7. Experts in modern personnel management generally agree that employees on all job levels should be permitted to offer suggestions for improving work methods.
Of the following, the CHIEF limitation of such suggestions is that they may, at times,

    A. be offered primarily for financial reward and not show genuine interest in improvement of work methods
    B. be directed towards making individual jobs easier
    C. be restricted by the employees' fear of radically changing the work methods favored by their supervisors
    D. show little awareness of the effects on the overall objectives and functions of the entire agency

7.\_\_\_

8. Through the supervisory process and relationship, the supervisor is trying to help workers gain increased self-awareness.
Of the following statements concerning this process, the one which is MOST accurate is:

    A. Self-awareness is developed gradually so that worker can learn to control his own reactions.
    B. Worker is expected to be introspective primarily for his own enlightenment.
    C. Supervisor is trying to help worker handle any emotional difficulties he may reveal.
    D. Worker is expected at the onset to share and determine with the supervisor what in his previous background makes it difficult for him to use certain ideas.

8.\_\_\_

9. The one of the following statements concerning principles in the learning process which is LEAST accurate is:

   A. Some degree of regression on the part of the worker is usually natural in the process of development and this should be accepted by the supervisor.
   B. When a beginning worker shows problems, the supervisor should first handle this behavior as a personality difficulty.
   C. It has been found in the work training process that some degree of resistance is usually inevitable.
   D. The emotional content of work practice may tend to set up *blind spots* in workers.

10. Of the following, the one that represents the BEST basis for planning the content of a successful staff development program is the

   A. time available for meetings
   B. chief social problems of the community
   C. common needs of the staff workers as related to the situations with which they are dealing
   D. experimental programs conducted by other agencies

11. In planning staff development seminars, the MOST valuable topics for discussion are likely to be those selected from

   A. staff suggestions based on the staff's interest and needs
   B. topics recommended for consideration by professional organizations
   C. topics selected by the administration based on demonstrated limitations of staff skill and knowledge
   D. topics selected by the administration based on a combination of staff interest and objectivity evaluated staff needs

12. Staff meetings designed to promote professional staff development are MOST likely to achieve this goal when

   A. there is the widest participation among all staff members who attend the meetings
   B. participation by the most skilled and experienced staff members is predominant
   C. participation by selected staff members is planned before the meeting sessions
   D. supervisory personnel take major responsibility for participation

13. Assume that you are the leader of a conference attended by representatives of various city and private agencies. After the conference has been underway for a considerable time, you realize that the representative of one of these agencies has said nothing. It would generally be BEST for you to

   A. ask him if he would like to say anything
   B. ask the group a pertinent question that he would probably be best able to answer
   C. make no special effort to include him in the conversation
   D. address the next question you planned to ask to him directly

14. A member of a decision-making conference generally makes his BEST contribution to the conference when he

   A. compromises on his own point of view and accepts most of the points of other conference members
   B. persuades the conference to accept all or most of his points

C. persuades the conference to accept his major proposals but will yield on the minor ones
D. succeeds in integrating his ideas with the ideas of the other conference members

15. Of the following, the LEAST accurate statement concerning the compilation and use of statistics in administration is:

    A. Interpretation of statistics is as necessary as their compilation.
    B. Statistical records of expenditures and services are one of the bases for budget preparation.
    C. Statistics on the quality of services rendered to the community will clearly delineate the human values achieved.
    D. The results achieved from collecting and compiling statistics must be in keeping with the cost and effort required.

16. An important administrative problem is how precisely to define the limits on authority that is delegated to subordinate supervisors.
    Such definition of limits of authority SHOULD be

    A. as precise as possible and practicable in all areas
    B. as precise as possible and practicable in all areas of function, but should allow considerable flexibility in the area of personnel management
    C. as precise as possible and practicable in the area of personnel management, but should allow considerable flexibility in the areas of function
    D. in general terms so as to allow considerable flexibility both in the areas of function and in the areas of personnel management

17. The LEAST important of the following reasons why a particular activity should be assigned to a unit which performs activities dissimilar to it is that

    A. close coordination is needed between the particular activity and other activities performed by the unit
    B. it will enhance the reputation and prestige of the unit supervisor
    C. the unit makes frequent use of the results of this particular activity
    D. the unit supervisor has a sound knowledge and understanding of the particular activity

18. The MOST important of the following reasons why the average resident of a deteriorated slum neighborhood resists relocation to an area in the suburbs with better physical accommodations is that he

    A. does not recognize as undesirable the characteristics which are responsible for deterioration of the neighborhood
    B. has some expectation of neighborly assistance in his old home in times of stress and adversity
    C. hopes for better days when he may be able to become a figure of some importance and envy in the old neighborhood
    D. is attuned to the noise of the city and fears the quiet of the suburb

19. From a psychological and sociological point of view, the MOST important of the following dangers to the persons living in an economically depressed area in which the only step taken by governmental and private social agencies to assist these persons is the granting of a dole is that

    A. industry will be reluctant to expand its operations in that area
    B. the dole will encourage additional non-producers to enter the area
    C. the residents of the area will probably have to find their own solution to their problems
    D. their permanent dependency will be fostered

19.____

20. The term *real wages* is GENERALLY used by economists to mean the

    A. amount of take-home pay left after taxes, social security, and other such deductions have been made by the employer
    B. average wage actually earned during a calendar or fiscal year
    C. family income expressed on a per capita basis
    D. wages expressed in terms of its buyer power

20.____

21. It has, at times, been suggested that an effective way to eradicate juvenile delinquency would be to arrest and punish the parents for the criminal actions of their delinquent children.
    The one of the following which is the CHIEF defect of this proposal is that

    A. it fails to get at the cause of the delinquent act and tends to further weaken disturbed parent-child relationships
    B. since the criminally inclined child has apparently demonstrated little love or affection for his parent, the child will be unlikely to amend his behavior in order to avoid hurting his parent
    C. the child who commits anti-social acts does so in many cases in order to hurt his parents so that this proposal would not only increase the parents' sorrow, but would also serve as an incentive to more delinquency by the child
    D. the punishment should be limited to the person who commits the illegal action rather than to those who are most interested in his welfare

21.____

22. Surveys which have compared the relative stability of marriages between white persons with marriages between non-white persons in this country have shown that, among Blacks, there is

    A. a significantly higher percentage of spouses absent from the household than among whites
    B. a significantly higher percentage of spouses absent from the household than among whites living in the South, but the opposite is true in the Northeast
    C. a significantly lower percentage of spouses absent from the household than among whites
    D. no significant difference in the percentage of spouses absent from the household when compared with the white population

22.____

23. A phenomenon found in the cultural and recreational patterns of European immigrant families in America is that, generally, the foreign-born adults

    A. as well as their children, tend soon to forget their old-world activities and adopt the cultural and recreational customs of America
    B. as well as their children, tend to retain and continue their old-world cultural and recreational pursuits, and find it equally difficult to adopt those of America
    C. tend soon to drop their old pursuits and adopt the cultural and recreational patterns of America while their children find it somewhat more difficult to make this change
    D. tend to retain and continue their old-world cultural and recreational pursuits while their children tend to rapidly replace these by the games and cultural patterns of America

24. Certain mores of migrant groups are strengthened under the impact of their contact with the native society while other mores are weakened.
    In the case of Puerto Ricans who have come to the city, the effect of such contact upon their traditional family structure has been a

    A. strengthening of the former maternalistic family structure
    B. strengthening of the former paternalistic family structure
    C. weakening of the former maternalistic family structure
    D. weakening of the former paternalistic family structure

25. Administrative reviews and special studies of independent experts, as reported by the Department of Health, Education and Welfare, indicate that the proportion of recipients of public assistance who receive such assistance through *wilful misrepresentation* of the facts is

    A. less than 1%  
    B. about 4%
    C. between 4% and 7%  
    D. between 7% and 10%

## KEY (CORRECT ANSWERS)

| | | | |
|---|---|---|---|
| 1. | B | 11. | D |
| 2. | D | 12. | A |
| 3. | D | 13. | B |
| 4. | B | 14. | D |
| 5. | A | 15. | C |
| 6. | B | 16. | A |
| 7. | D | 17. | B |
| 8. | A | 18. | B |
| 9. | B | 19. | D |
| 10. | C | 20. | D |

21. A
22. A
23. D
24. D
25. A

# TEST 2

DIRECTIONS: Each question or incomplete statement is followed by several suggested answers or completions. Select the one that BEST answers the question or completes the statement. *PRINT THE LETTER OF THE CORRECT ANSWER IN THE SPACE AT THE RIGHT.*

1. In order to meet more adequately the public assistance needs occasioned by sudden changes in the national economy, social service agencies, in general, recommend, as a matter of preference, that

   A. each locality build up reserve funds to care for needy unemployed persons in order to avoid a breakdown of local resources such as occurred during the depression
   B. the federal government assume total responsibility for the administration of public assistance
   C. state settlement laws be strictly enforced so that unemployed workers will be encouraged to move from the emergency industry centers to their former homes
   D. a federal-state-local program of general assistance be established with need as the only eligibility requirement
   E. eligibility requirements be tightened to assure that only legitimately worthy local residents receive the available assistance

2. The MOST practical method of maintaining income for the majority of aged persons who are no longer able to work, or for the families of those workers who are deceased, is a(n)

   A. comprehensive system of non-categorical assistance on a basis of cash payments
   B. integrated system of public assistance and extensive work relief programs
   C. co-ordinated system of providing care in institutions and foster homes
   D. system of contributory insurance in which a cash benefit is paid as a matter of right
   E. expanded system of diagnostic and treatment centers

3. With the establishment of insurance and assistance programs under the Social Security Act, many institutional programs for the aged have tended to the greatest extent toward an increased emphasis on providing, of the following types of assistance,

   A. care for the aged by denominational groups
   B. care for children requiring institutional treatment
   C. recreational facilities for the able-bodied aged
   D. training facilities in industrial homework for the aged
   E. care for the chronically ill and infirm aged

4. Of the following terms, the one which BEST describes the Social Security Act is

   A. enabling legislation
   B. regulatory statute
   C. appropriations act
   D. act of mandamus
   E. provisional enactment

5. Of the following, the term which MOST accurately describes an appropriation is

   A. authority to spend
   B. itemized estimate
   C. *fund* accounting
   D. anticipated expenditure
   E. executive budget

6. When business expansion causes a demand for labor, the worker group which benefits MOST immediately is the group comprising

   A. employed workers
   B. inexperienced workers under 21 years of age
   C. experienced workers 21 to 25 years of age
   D. inexperienced older workers
   E. experienced workers over 40 years of age

7. The MOST important failure in our present system of providing social work services in local communities is the

   A. absence of adequate facilities for treating mental illness
   B. lack of coordination of available data and service in the community
   C. poor quality of the casework services provided by the public agencies
   D. limitations of the probation and parole services
   E. inadequacy of private family welfare services

8. Recent studies of the relationship between incidence of illness and the use of available treatment services among various population groups in the United States show that

   A. while lower-income families use medical services with greater frequency, total expenditures are greater among the upper-income groups
   B. although the average duration of a period of medical care increases with increasing income, the average frequency of obtaining care decreases with increasing income
   C. adequacy of medical service is inversely related to frequency of illness and size of family income
   D. families in the higher-income brackets have a heavier incidence of illness and make greater use of medical services than do those in the lower-income brackets
   E. both as to frequency and duration, the distribution of illness falls equally on all groups, but the use of medical services increases with income

9. The category of disease which most public health departments and authorities usually are NOT equipped to handle *directly* is that of

   A. chronic disease
   B. bronchial disturbances
   C. venereal disease
   D. mosquito-borne diseases
   E. incipient forms of tuberculosis

10. Recent statistical analyses of the causes of death in the United States indicate that medical science has now reached the stage where it would be preferable to increase its research toward control, among the following, PRINCIPALLY of

   A. accidents
   B. suicides
   C. communicable disease
   D. chronic disease
   E. infant mortality

11. Although the distinction between mental disease and mental deficiency is fairly definite, both these conditions USUALLY represent

   A. diseases of one part or organ of the body rather than of the whole person
   B. an inadequacy existing from birth or shortly afterwards and appearing as a simplicity of intelligence
   C. a deficiency developing later in life and characterized by distortions of attitude and belief
   D. inadequacies in meeting life situations and in conducting one's affairs
   E. somewhat transitory conditions characterized by disturbances of consciousness

12. According to studies made by reliable medical research organizations in the United States, differences among the states in proportion of physicians to population are MOST directly related to the

   A. geographic resources among the states
   B. skill of the physicians
   C. relative proportions of urban and rural people in the population of the states
   D. number of specialists in the ranks of the physicians
   E. health status of the people in the various states

13. One of the MAIN advantages of incorporating a charitable organization is that

   A. gifts or property of a corporation cannot be held in perpetuity
   B. gifts to unincorporated charitable organizations are not deductible from the taxable income
   C. incorporation gives less legal standing or *personality* than an informal partnership
   D. members of a corporation cannot be held liable for debts contracted by the organization
   E. a corporate organization cannot be sued

14. The BASIC principle underlying a social security program is that the government should provide

   A. aid to families that is not dependent on state or local participation
   B. assistance to any worthy family unable to maintain itself independently
   C. protection to individuals against some of the social risks that are inherent in an industrialized society
   D. safeguards against those factors leading to economic depression

15. The activities of state and local public welfare agencies are dependent to a large degree on the public assistance program of the federal government.
    The one of the following which the federal government has NOT been successful in achieving within the local agencies is the

    A. broadening of the scope of public assistance administration
    B. expansion of the categorical programs
    C. improvement of the quality of service given to clients
    D. standardization of the administration of general assistance programs

16. Of the following statements, the one which BEST describes the federal government's position, as stated in the Social Security Act, with regard to tests of character or fitness to be administered by local or state welfare departments to prospective clients is that

    A. no tests of character are required but they are not specifically prohibited
    B. if tests of character are used, they must be uniform throughout the state
    C. tests of character are contrary to the philosophy of the federal government and are to be considered illegal
    D. no tests of character are required, and assistance to those states that use them will be withheld

17. An increase in the size of the welfare grant may increase the cost of the welfare program not only in terms of those already on the welfare rolls, but because it may result in an increase in the number of people on the rolls.
    The CHIEF reason that an increase in the size of the grant may cause an increase in the number of people on the rolls is that the increased grant may

    A. induce low-salaried wage earners to apply for assistance rather than continue at their menial jobs
    B. make eligible for assistance many people whose resources are just above the previous standard
    C. induce many people to apply for assistance who hesitated to do so because of meagerness of the previous grant
    D. make relatives less willing to contribute because the welfare grant can more adequately cover their dependents' needs

18. One of the MAIN differences between the use of casework methods by a public welfare agency and by a private welfare agency is that the public welfare agency

    A. requires that the applicant be eligible for the services it offers
    B. cannot maintain a non-judgmental attitude toward its clients because of legal requirements
    C. places less emphasis on efforts to change the behavior of its clients
    D. must be more objective in its approach to the client because public funds are involved

19. All definitions of social casework include certain major assumptions.
    Of the following, the one which is NOT considered a major assumption is that

    A. the individual and society are interdependent
    B. social forces influence behavior and attitudes, affording opportunity for self-development and contribution to the world in which we live
    C. reconstruction of the total personality and reorganization of the total environment are specific goals
    D. the client is a responsible participant at every step in the solution of his problems

20. In order to provide those services to problem families which will help restore them to a self-maintaining status, it is necessary to FIRST

    A. develop specific plans to meet the individual needs of the problem family
    B. reduce the size of those caseloads composed of multi-problem families
    C. remove them from their environment and provide them with the means of overcoming their dependency
    D. identify the factors causing their dependency and creating problems for them

21. Of the following, the type of service which can provide the client with the MOST enduring help is that service which

    A. provides him with material aid and relieves the stress of his personal problems
    B. assists him to do as much as he can for himself and leaves him free to make his own decisions
    C. directs his efforts towards returning to a self-maintaining status and provides him with desirable goals
    D. gives him the feeling that the agency is interested in him as an individual and stands ready to assist him with his problems

22. Psychiatric interpretation of unconscious motivations can bring childhood conflicts into the framework of adult understanding and open the way for them to be resolved, but the interpretation must come from within the client.
    This statement means MOST NEARLY that

    A. treatment is merely diagnosis in reverse
    B. explaining a client to himself will lead to the resolution of his problems
    C. the client must arrive at an understanding of his problems
    D. unresolved childhood conflicts create problems for the adult

23. A significant factor in the United States economic picture is the state of the labor market. Of the following, the MOST important development affecting the labor market has been

    A. an expansion of the national defense effort creating new plant capacity
    B. the general increase in personal income as a result of an increase in overtime pay in manufacturing industries
    C. the growth of manufacturing as a result of automation
    D. a demand for a large number of jobs resulting from new job applicants as well as from displacement of workers by automation

24. A typical characteristic of the United States population over 65 is that MOST of them

    A. are independent and capable of self-support
    B. live in their own homes but require various supportive services
    C. live in institutions for the aged
    D. require constant medical attention at home or in an institution

25. The one of the following factors which is MOST important in preventing persons 65 years of age and older from getting employment is the

    A. misconceptions by employers of skills and abilities of senior citizens
    B. lack of skill in modern industrial techniques of persons in this age group
    C. social security laws restricting employment of persons in this age group
    D. unwillingness of persons in this age group to continue supporting themselves

# KEY (CORRECT ANSWERS)

| | | | |
|---|---|---|---|
| 1. | D | 11. | D |
| 2. | D | 12. | C |
| 3. | E | 13. | D |
| 4. | A | 14. | C |
| 5. | A | 15. | D |
| 6. | B | 16. | A |
| 7. | B | 17. | B |
| 8. | C | 18. | C |
| 9. | A | 19. | C |
| 10. | D | 20. | D |

21. B
22. C
23. D
24. B
25. A

# EXAMINATION SECTION
## TEST 1

DIRECTIONS: Each question or incomplete statement is followed by several suggested answers or completions. Select the one that BEST answers the question or completes the statement. *PRINT THE LETTER OF THE CORRECT ANSWER IN THE SPACE AT THE RIGHT.*

1. In public agencies, communications should be based PRIMARILY on a
   A. two-way flow from the top down and from the bottom up, most of which should be given in writing to avoid ambiguity
   B. multi-direction flow among all levels and with outside persons
   C. rapid, internal one-way flow from the top down
   D. two-way flow of information, most of which should be given orally for purposes of clarity

2. In some organizations, changes in policy or procedures are often communicated by word of mouth from supervisors to employees with no prior discussion or exchange of viewpoints with employees.
   This procedure often produces employee dissatisfaction CHIEFLY because
   A. information is mostly unusable since a considerable amount of time is required to transmit information
   B. lower-level supervisors tend to be excessively concerned with minor details
   C. management has failed to seek employees' advice before making changes
   D. valuable staff time is lost between decision-making and the implementation of decisions

3. For good letter writing, you should try to visualize the person to whom you are writing, especially if you know him.
   Of the following rules, it is LEAST helpful in such visualization to think of
   A. the person's likes and dislikes, his concerns, and his needs
   B. what you would be likely to say if speaking in person
   C. what you would expect to be asked if speaking in person
   D. your official position in order to be certain that your words are proper

4. One approach to good informal letter writing is to make letters and conversational.
   All of the following practices will usually help to do this EXCEPT:
   A. If possible, use a style which is similar to the style used when speaking
   B. Substitute phrases for single words (e.g., *at the present time for now*)
   C. Use contractions of words (e.g., *you're* for *you are*)
   D. Use ordinary vocabulary when possible

5. All of the following rules will aid in producing clarity in report-writing EXCEPT:
   A. Give specific details or examples, if possible
   B. Keep related words close together in each sentence
   C. Present information in sequential order
   D. Put several thoughts or ideas in each paragraph

6. The one of the following statements about public relations which is MOST accurate is that
   A. in the long run, appearance gains better results than performance
   B. objectivity is decreased if outside public relations consultants are employed
   C. public relations is the responsibility of every employee
   D. public relations should be based on a formal publicity program

7. The form of communication which is usually considered to be MOST personally directed to the intended recipient is the
   A. brochure    B. film    C. letter    D. radio

8. In general, a document that presents an organization's views or opinions on a particular topic is MOST accurately known as a
   A. tear sheet              B. position paper
   C. flyer                   D. journal

9. Assume that you have been asked to speak before an organization of persons who oppose a newly announced program in which you are involved. You feel tense about talking to this group.
   Which of the following rules generally would be MOST useful in gaining rapport when speaking before the audience?
   A. Impress them with your experience
   B. Stress all areas of disagreement
   C. Talk to the group as to one person
   D. Use formal grammar and language

10. An organization must have an effective public relations program since, at its best, public relations is a bridge to change.
    All of the following statements about communication and human behavior have validity EXCEPT:
    A. People are more likely to talk about controversial matters with like-minded people than with those holding other views
    B. The earlier an experience, the more powerful its effect since it influences how later experiences will be interpreted
    C. In periods of social tension, official sources gain increased believability
    D. Those who are already interested in a topic are the ones who are most open to receive new communications about it

11. An employee should be encouraged to talk easily and frankly when he is dealing with his supervisor.
    In order to encourage such free communication, it would be MOST appropriate for a supervisor to behave in a(n)
    A. sincere manner; assure the employee that you will deal with him honestly and openly
    B. official manner; you are a supervisor and must always act formally with subordinates
    C. investigative manner; you must probe and question to get to a basis of trust
    D. unemotional manner; the employee's emotions and background should play no part in your dealings with him

11.____

12. Research findings show that an increase in free communication within an agency GENERALLY results in which one of the following?
    A. Improved morale and productivity
    B. Increased promotional opportunities
    C. An increase in authority
    D. A spirit of honesty

12.____

13. Assume that you are a supervisor and your superiors have given you a new-type procedure to be followed.
    Before passing this information on to your subordinates, the one of the following actions that you should take FIRST is to
    A. ask your superiors to send out a memorandum to the entire staff
    B. clarify the procedure in your own mind
    C. set up a training course to provide instruction on the new procedure
    D. write a memorandum to your subordinates

13.____

14. Communication is necessary for an organization to be effective.
    The one of the following which is LEAST important for most communication systems is that
    A. messages are sent quickly and directly to the person who needs them to operate
    B. information should be conveyed understandably and accurately
    C. the method used to transmit information should be kept secret so that security can be maintained
    D. senders of messages must know how their messages are received and acted upon

14.____

15. Which one of the following is the CHIEF advantage of listening willingly to subordinates and encouraging them to talk freely and honestly?
    It
    A. reveals to supervisors the degree to which ideas that are passed down are accepted by subordinates
    B. reduces the participation of subordinates in the operation of the department
    C. encourages subordinates to try for promotion
    D. enables supervisors to learn more readily what the *grapevine* is saying

15.____

16. A supervisor may be informed through either oral or written reports.  16.____
Which one of the following is an ADVANTAGE of using oral reports?
    A. There is no need for a formal record of the report.
    B. An exact duplicate of the report is not easily transmitted to others.
    C. A good oral report requires little time for preparation.
    D. An oral report involves two-way communication between a subordinate and his supervisor.

17. Of the following, the MOST important reason why supervisors should communicate effectively with the public is to  17.____
    A. improve the public's understanding of information that is important for them to know
    B. establish a friendly relationship
    C. obtain information about the kinds of people who come to the agency
    D. convince the public that services are adequate

18. Supervisors should generally NOT use phrases like *too hard*, *too easy*, and *a lot* PRINCIPALLY because such phrases  18.____
    A. may be offensive to some minority groups
    B. are too informal
    C. mean different things to different people
    D. are difficult to remember

19. The ability to communicate clearly and concisely is an important element in effective leadership.  19.____
Which of the following statements about oral and written communication is GENERALLY true?
    A. Oral communication is more time-consuming.
    B. Written communication is more likely to be misinterpreted.
    C. Oral communication is useful only in emergencies.
    D. Written communication is useful mainly when giving information to fewer than twenty people.

20. Rumors can often have harmful and disruptive effects on an organization.  20.____
Which one of the following is the BEST way to prevent rumors from becoming a problem?
    A. Refuse to act on rumors, thereby making them less believable.
    B. Increase the amount of information passed along by the *grapevine*.
    C. Distribute as much factual information as possible.
    D. Provide training in report writing.

21. Suppose that a subordinate asks you about a rumor he has heard. The rumor deals with a subject which your superiors consider *confidential*.  21.____
Which of the following BEST describes how you should answer the subordinate? Tell

A. the subordinate that you don't make the rules and that he should speak to higher ranking officials
B. the subordinate that you will ask your superior for information
C. him only that you cannot comment on the matter
D. him the rumor is not true

22. Supervisors often find it difficult to *get their message across* when instructing newly appointed employees in their various duties.
The MAIN reason for this is generally that the
    A. duties of the employees have increased
    B. supervisor is often so expert in his area that he fails to see it from the learner's point of view
    C. supervisor adapts his instruction to the slowest learner in the group
    D. new employees are younger, less concerned with job security and more interested in fringe benefits

22.____

23. Assume that you are discussing a job problem with an employee under your supervision. During the discussion, you see that the man's eyes are turning away from you and that he is not paying attention.
In order to get the man's attention, you should FIRST
    A. ask him to look you in the eye
    B. talk to him about sports
    C. tell him he is being very rude
    D. change your tone of voice

23.____

24. As a supervisor, you may find it necessary to conduct meetings with your subordinates.
Of the following, which would be MOST helpful in assuring that a meeting accomplishes the purpose for which it was called?
    A. Give notice of the conclusions you would like to reach at the start of the meeting.
    B. Delay the start of the meeting until everyone is present.
    C. Write down points to be discussed in proper sequence.
    D. Make sure everyone is clear on whatever conclusions have been reached and on what must be done after the meeting.

24.____

25. Every supervisor will occasionally be called upon to deliver a reprimand to a subordinate. If done properly, this can greatly help an employee improve his performance.
Which one of the following is NOT a good practice to follow when giving a reprimand?
    A. Maintain your composure and temper
    B. Reprimand a subordinate in the presence of other employees so they can learn the same lesson
    C. Try to understand why the employee was not able to perform satisfactorily
    D. Let your knowledge of the man involved determine the exact nature of the reprimand

25.____

## KEY (CORRECT ANSWERS)

| | | | | |
|---|---|---|---|---|
| 1. | C | | 11. | A |
| 2. | B | | 12. | A |
| 3. | D | | 13. | B |
| 4. | B | | 14. | C |
| 5. | D | | 15. | A |
| | | | | |
| 6. | C | | 16. | D |
| 7. | C | | 17. | A |
| 8. | B | | 18. | C |
| 9. | C | | 19. | B |
| 10. | C | | 20. | C |

21. B
22. B
23. D
24. D
25. B

# TEST 2

DIRECTIONS: Each question or incomplete statement is followed by several suggested answers or completions. Select the one that BEST answers the question or completes the statement. *PRINT THE LETTER OF THE CORRECT ANSWER IN THE SPACE AT THE RIGHT.*

1. Usually one thinks of communication as a single step, essentially that of transmitting an idea.
   Actually, however, this is only part of a total process, the FIRST step of which should be
   A. the prompt dissemination of the idea to those who may be affected by it
   B. motivating those affected to take the required action
   C. clarifying the idea in one's own mind
   D. deciding to whom the idea is to be communicated

   1.____

2. Research studies on patterns of informal communication have concluded that most individuals in a group tend to be passive recipients of news, while a few make it their business to spread it around in an organization.
   With this conclusion in mind, it would be MOST correct for the supervisor to attempt to identify these few individuals and
   A. give them the complete facts on important matters in advance of others
   B. inform the other subordinates of the identity of these few individuals so that their influence may be minimized
   C. keep them straight on the facts on important matters
   D. warn them to cease passing along any information to others

   2.____

3. The one of the following which is the PRINCIPAL advantage of making an oral report is that it
   A. affords an immediate opportunity for two-way communication between the subordinate and superior
   B. is an easy method for the superior to use in transmitting information to others of equal rank
   C. saves the time of all concerned
   D. permits more precise pinpointing of praise or blame by means of follow-up questions by the superior

   3.____

4. An agency may sometimes undertake a public relations program of a defensive nature.
   With reference to the use of defensive public relations, it would be MOST correct to state that it
   A. is bound to be ineffective since defensive statements, even though supported by factual data, can never hope to even partly overcome the effects of prior unfavorable attacks
   B. proves that the agency has failed to establish good relationships with newspapers, radio stations, or other means of publicity

   4.____

C. shows that the upper echelons of the agency have failed to develop sound public relations procedures and techniques
D. is sometimes required to aid morale by protecting the agency from unjustified criticism and misunderstanding of policies or procedures

5. Of the following factors which contribute to possible undesirable public attitudes towards an agency, the one which is MOST susceptible to being changed by the efforts of the individual employee in an organization is that
    A. enforcement of unpopular regulations as offended many individuals
    B. the organization itself has an unsatisfactory reputation
    C. the public is not interested in agency matters
    D. there are many errors in judgment committed by individual subordinates

6. It is not enough for an agency's services to be of a high quality; attention must also be given to the acceptability of these services to the general public.
This statement is GENERALLY
    A. *false*; a superior quality of service automatically wins public support
    B. *true*; the agency cannot generally progress beyond the understanding and support of the public
    C. *false*; the acceptance by the public of agency services determines their quality
    D. *true*; the agency is generally unable to engage in any effective enforcement activity without public support

7. Sustained agency participation in a program sponsored by a community organization is MOST justified when
    A. the achievement of agency objectives in some area depends partly on the activity of this organization
    B. the community organization is attempting to widen the base of participation in all community affairs
    C. the agency is uncertain as to what the community wants
    D. the agency is uncertain as to what the community wants

8. Of the following, the LEAST likely way in which a records system may serve a supervisor is in
    A. developing a sympathetic and cooperative public attitude toward the agency
    B. improving the quality of supervision by permitting a check on the accomplishment of subordinates
    C. permit a precise prediction of the exact incidences in specific categories for the following year
    D. helping to take the guesswork out of the distribution of the agency

9. Assuming that the *grapevine* in any organization is virtually indestructible, the one of the following which it is MOST important for management to understand is:
   A. What is being spread by means of the *grapevine* and the reason for spreading it
   B. What is being spread by means of the *grapevine* and how it is being spread
   C. Who is involved in spreading the information that is on the *grapevine*
   D. Why those who are involved in spreading the information are doing so

10. When the supervisor writes a report concerning an investigation to which he has been assigned, it should be LEAST intended to provide
    A. a permanent official record of relevant information gathered
    B. a summary of case findings limited to facts which tend to indicate the guilt of a suspect
    C. a statement of the facts on which higher authorities may base a corrective or disciplinary action
    D. other investigators with information so that they may continue with other phases of the investigation

11. In survey work, questionnaires rather than interviews are sometimes used. The one of the following which is a DISADVANTAGE of the questionnaire method as compared with the interview is the
    A. difficulty of accurately interpreting the results
    B. problem of maintaining anonymity of the participant
    C. fact that it is relatively uneconomical
    D. requirement of special training for the distribution of questionnaires

12. in his contacts with the public, an employee should attempt to create a good climate of support for his agency.
    This statement is GENERALLY
    A. *false*; such attempts are clearly beyond the scope of his responsibility
    B. *true*; employees of an agency who come in contact with the public have the opportunity to affect public relations
    C. *false*; such activity should be restricted to supervisors trained in public relations techniques
    D. *true*; the future expansion of the agency depends to a great extent on continued public support of the agency

13. The repeated use by a supervisor of a call for volunteers to get a job done is objectionable MAINLY because it
    A. may create a feeling of animosity between the volunteers and the non-volunteers
    B. may indicate that the supervisor is avoiding responsibility for making assignments which will be most productive
    C. is an indication that the supervisor is not familiar with the individual capabilities of his men
    D. is unfair to men who, for valid reasons, do not, or cannot volunteer

14. Of the following statements concerning subordinates' expressions to a supervisor of their opinions and feelings concerning work situations, the one which is MOST correct is that
    A. by listening and responding to such expressions the supervisor encourages the development of complaints
    B. the lack of such expressions should indicate to the supervisor that there is a high level of job satisfaction
    C. the more the supervisor listens to and responds to such expressions, the more he demonstrates lack of supervisory ability
    D. by listening and responding to such expressions, the supervisor will enable many subordinates to understand and solve their own problems on the job

15. In attempting to motivate employees, rewards are considered preferable to punishment PRIMARILY because
    A. punishment seldom has any effect on human behavior
    B. punishment usually results in decreased production
    C. supervisors find it difficult to punish
    D. rewards are more likely to result in willing cooperation

16. In an attempt to combat the low morale in his organization, a high level supervisor publicized an *open-door policy* to allow employees who wished to do so to come to him with their complaints.
    Which of the following is LEAST likely to account for the fact that no employee came in with a complaint?
    A. Employees are generally reluctant to go over the heads of their immediate supervisor.
    B. The employees did not feel that management would help them.
    C. The low morale was not due to complaints associated with the job.
    D. The employees felt that they had more to lose than to gain.

17. It is MOST desirable to use written instructions rather than oral instructions for a particular job when
    A. a mistake on the job will not be serious
    B. the job can be completed in a short time
    C. there is no need to explain the job minutely
    D. the job involves many details

18. If you receive a telephone call regarding a matter which your office does not handle, you should FIRST
    A. give the caller the telephone number of the proper office so that he can dial again
    B. offer to transfer the caller to the proper office
    C. suggest that the caller re-dial since he probably dialed incorrectly
    D. tell the caller he has reached the wrong office and then hang up

19. When you answer the telephone, the MOST important reason for identifying yourself and your organization is to
    A. give the caller time to collect his or her thoughts
    B. impress the caller with your courtesy
    C. inform the caller that he or she has reached the right number
    D. set a business-like tone at the beginning of the conversation

19.____

20. As soon as you pick up the phone, a very angry caller begins immediately to complain about city agencies and *red tape*. He says that he has been shifted to two or three different offices. It turs out that he is seeking information which is not immediately available to you. You believe, you know, however, where it can be found.
    Which of the following actions is the BEST one for you to take?
    A. To eliminate all confusion, suggest that the caller write the agency stating explicitly what he wants.
    B. Apologize by telling the caller how busy city agencies now are, but also tell him directly that you do not have the information he needs.
    C. Ask for the caller's telephone number and assure him you will call back after you have checked further.
    D. Give the caller the name and telephone number of the person who might be able to help, but explain that you are not positive he will get results/

20.____

21. Which of the following approaches usually provides the BEST communication in the objectives and values of a new program which is to be introduced?
    A. A general written description of the program by the program manager for review by those who share responsibility
    B. An effective verbal presentation by the program manager to those affected
    C. Development of the plan and operational approach in carrying out the program by the program manager assisted by his key subordinates
    D. Development of the plan by the program manager's supervisor

21.____

22. What is the BEST approach for introducing change?
    A
    A. combination of written and also verbal communication to all personnel affected by the change
    B. general bulletin to all personnel
    C. meeting pointing out all the values of the new approach
    D. written directive to key personnel

22.____

23. Of the following, committees are BEST used for
    A. advising the head of the organization
    B. improving functional work
    C. making executive decisions
    D. making specific planning decisions

23.____

24. An effective discussion leader is one who
    A. announces the problem and his preconceived solution at the start of the discussion
    B. guides and directs the discussion according to pre-arranged outline
    C. interrupts or corrects confused participants to save time
    D. permits anyone to say anything at any time

25. The human relations movement in management theory is basically concerned with
    A. counteracting employee unrest
    B. eliminating the *time and motion* man
    C. interrelationships among individuals in organizations
    D. the psychology of the worker

# KEY (CORRECT ANSWERS)

| | | | |
|---|---|---|---|
| 1. | C | 11. | A |
| 2. | C | 12. | B |
| 3. | A | 13. | B |
| 4. | D | 14. | D |
| 5. | D | 15. | D |
| 6. | B | 16. | C |
| 7. | A | 17. | D |
| 8. | C | 18. | B |
| 9. | A | 19. | C |
| 10. | B | 20. | C |

21. C
22. A
23. A
24. B
25. C

# REPORT WRITING

# EXAMINATION SECTION

## TEST 1

DIRECTIONS: Each question or incomplete statement is followed by several suggested answers or completions. Select the one that BEST answers the question or completes the statement. *PRINT THE LETTER OF THE CORRECT ANSWER IN THE SPACE AT THE RIGHT.*

Questions 1-5.

DIRECTIONS: Questions 1 through 5 are to be answered on the basis of the Report of Offense that appears below.'

| REPORT OF OFFENSE | Report No. <u>26743</u> |
|---|---|
| | Date of Report <u>10-12</u> |
| Inmate *Joseph Brown* | |
| Age *27* | Number *61274* |
| Sentence *90 days* | Assignment *KU-187* |
| Place of offense *R.P.W. 4-1* | Date of offense *10/11/* |
| Offense <u>Assaulting inmate</u> | |
| Details *During 9:00 P.M., cellblock cleanup, inmate John Jones asked for pail being used by Brown. Brown refused. Correction officer requested that Brown comply. Brown then threw pail at Jones with intent to injure him and said he would "get" Jones. Jones not hurt.* | |
| Force used by officer *None* | |
| Name of reporting officer *R. Rodriguez* | No. *C-2056* |
| Name of superior officer *P. Ferguson* | |

1. The person who made out this report is
   A. Joseph Brown  B. John Jones
   C. R. Rodriguez  D. P. Ferguson

   1.____

2. Disregarding the details, the specific offense reported was
   A. insulting a fellow inmate  B. assaulting a fellow inmate
   C. injuring a fellow inmate  D. disobeying a correct officer

   2.____

3. The number of the inmate who committed the offense is
   A. 26743  B. 61274  C. KU-187  D. CJ-2056

   3.____

4. The offense took place on
   A. October 11  B. June 12  C. December 10  D. November 13

   4.____

5. The place where the offense occurred is identified in the report as
   A. Brown's cell  B. Jones' cell  C. KU-187  D. R.P.W., 4-1

   5.____

Questions 6-10.

DIRECTIONS: Questions 6 through 10 are to be answered on the basis of the Report of Loss or Theft that appears below.

| REPORT OF LOSS OR THEFT | Date: *12/4* | Time: *9:15 A.M.* |
|---|---|---|
| Complaint made by: *Richard Aldridge* *306 S. Walter St.* | ☐ Owner ☒ Other – explain: *Head of Acctg. Dept.* | |
| Type of Property: *Computer* | | Value: *$450.00* |
| Description: Dell Inspiron laptop | | |
| Location: *768 N. Margin Ave., Accounting Dept. 3rd Floor* | | |
| Time: *Overnight 12/3 – 12/4* | | |
| Circumstances: *Mr. Aldridge reports he arrived at work 8:45 A.M., found office door open and machine missing. Nothing else reported missing. I investigated and found signs of forced entry; door lock was broken.* | | |
| Signature of Reporting Officer: *B.L. Ramirez* | | |
| Notify: | | |
| ☐ Q Building & Grounds Office, 768 N. Margin Ave. | | |
| ☐ Q Lost Property Office, 110 Brand Ave. 0 | | |
| ☒ Security Office, 703 N. Wide Street | | |

6. The person who made this complaint is
   A. a secretary
   B. a security officer
   C. Richard Aldridge
   D. B.L. Ramirez

7. The report concerns a computer that has been
   A. lost   B. damaged   C. stolen   D. sold

8. The person who took the computer PROBABLY entered the office through
   A. a door
   B. a window
   C. the roof
   D. the basement

9. When did the head of the Accounting Department FIRST notice that the computer was missing?
   A. December 4 at 9:15 A.M.
   B. December 4 at 8:45 A.M.
   C. The night of December 3
   D. The night of December 4

10. The event described in the report took place at
    A. 306 South Walter Street
    B. 768 North Margin Avenue
    C. 110 Brand Avenue
    D. 703 North Wide Street

Questions 11-15.

DIRECTIONS: Questions 11 through 15 are to be answered on the basis of the following excerpt from a recorded Annual Report of the Police Department. This material should be read first and then referred to in answering these questions, which are to be answered SOLELY on the basis of the material herein contained.

## LEGAL BUREAU

One of the more important functions of this bureau is to analyze and furnish the department with pertinent information concerning Federal and State statutes and local laws which affect the department, law enforcement or crime prevention. In addition, all measures introduced in the State Legislature and the City Council, which may affect this department, are carefully reviewed by members of the Legal Bureau and, where necessary, opinions and recommendations thereon are prepared.

Another important function of this office is the prosecution of cases in the Magistrate's Courts. This is accomplished by assignment of attorneys who are members of the Legal Bureau to appear in those cases which are deemed to raise issues of importance to the department or questions of law which require technical presentation to facilitate proper determination; and also in those cases where request is made for such appearance by a magistrate, some other official of the city, or a member of the force. Attorneys are regularly assigned to prosecute all cases in the Family Court.

Proposed legislation was prepared and sponsored for introduction in the State Legislature and, at this writing, one of these proposals has already been enacted into law and five others are presently on the Governor's desk awaiting executive action. The new law prohibits the sale or possession of a hypodermic syringe or needle by an unauthorized person. The bureau's proposals awaiting executive action pertain to: an amendment to the Code of Criminal Procedure prohibiting desk officers from taking bail in gambling cases or in cases mentioned in Section 552, Code of Criminal Procedure, including confidence men and swindlers as jostlers in the Penal Law; prohibiting the sale of switch-blade knives of any size to children under 16 and bills extending the licensing period of gunsmiths.

The Legal Bureau has regularly cooperated with the Corporation Counsel and the District attorneys in respect to matters affecting this department, and has continued to advise and represent the Police Athletic League, the Police Sports Association, the Police Relief Fund, and the Police Pension Fund.

The following is a statistical report of the activities of the bureau during the current year as compared with the previous year:

|  | Current Year | Previous Year |
|---|---|---|
| Memoranda of law prepared | 68 | 83 |
| Legal matters forwarded to Corporation Counsel | 122 | 144 |
| Letters requesting legal information | 756 | 807 |
| Letters requesting departmental records | 139 | 111 |
| Matters for publication | 17 | 26 |
| Court appearances of members of bureau | 4,678 | 4,621 |
| Conferences | 94 | 103 |
| Lectures at Police Academy | 30 | 33 |
| Reports on proposed legislation | 194 | 255 |
| Deciphering of codes | 79 | 27 |
| Expert testimony | 31 | 16 |
| Notices to court witnesses | 55 | 81 |
| Briefs prepared | 22 | 18 |
| Court papers prepared | 258 | — |

11. One of the functions of the Legal Bureau is to
    A. review and make recommendations on proposed federal laws affecting law enforcement
    B. prepare opinions on all measures introduced in the state legislature and the City Council
    C. furnish the Police Department with pertinent information concerning all new federal and state laws
    D. analyze all laws affecting the work of the Police Department

11.____

12. The Legal Bureau sponsored a bill that would
    A. extend the licenses of gunsmiths
    B. prohibit the sale of switch-blade knives to children of any size
    C. place confidence men and swindlers in the same category as jostlers in the Penal Law
    D. prohibit desk officers from admitting gamblers, confidence men, and swindlers to bail

12.____

13. From the report, it is NOT reasonable to infer that
    A. fewer bills affecting the Police Department were introduced in the current year
    B. the preparation of court papers was a new activity assumed in the current year
    C. the Code of Criminal Procedure authorizes desk officers to accept bail in certain cases
    D. the penalty for jostling and swindling is the same

13.____

14. According to the statistical report, the activity showing the GREATEST percentage of decrease in the current year compared with the previous year was
    A. matters for publication
    B. reports on proposed legislation
    C. notices to court witnesses
    D. memoranda of law prepared

14.____

15. According to the report, the percentage of bills prepared and sponsored by the Legal Bureau, which were passed by the State Legislature and sent to the Governor for approval, was
    A. approximately 3.2%
    B. approximately 2.6%
    C. approximately .5%
    D. not capable of determination from the data given

15.____

## KEY (CORRECT ANSWERS)

| | | | | | |
|---|---|---|---|---|---|
| 1. | C | 6. | C | 11. | D |
| 2. | B | 7. | C | 12. | C |
| 3. | B | 8. | A | 13. | D |
| 4. | A | 9. | B | 14. | A |
| 5. | D | 10. | B | 15. | D |

# TEST 2

DIRECTIONS: Each question or incomplete statement is followed by several suggested answers or completions. Select the one that BEST answers the question or completes the statement. *PRINT THE LETTER OF THE CORRECT ANSWER IN THE SPACE AT THE RIGHT.*

Questions 1-2.

DIRECTIONS: Questions 1 and 2 are to be answered on the basis of the Instructions, the Bridge and Tunnel Officer's Toll Report form, and the situation given below. The questions ask how the report form should be filled in based on the Instructions and the information given in the situation.

## INSTRUCTIONS

Assume that a Bridge and Tunnel Officer on duty in a toll booth must make an entry on the following report form immediately after each incident in which a vehicle driver does not pay the correct toll.

| BRIDGE AND TUNNEL OFFICER'S TOLL REPORT | | | |
|---|---|---|---|
| Officer_____ | | Date_____ | |
| Time | Type of Vehicle | Toll Collected | Explanation of Entry |
| 1._____ | _____ | _____ | _____ |
| 2._____ | _____ | _____ | _____ |
| _____ | _____ | _____ | _____ |

## SITUATION

John McDonald is a Bridge and Tunnel Officer assigned to toll booth 4, between the hours of 11 P.M. and 1 A.M.. On this particular tour, two incidents occurred. At 11:43 P.M., a five-axle truck stopped at the toll booth and Officer McDonald collected a $2.50 toll from the driver. As the truck passed, he realized the toll should have been $3.30, and he quickly copied the vehicle's license plate number as M724HJ. At 12:35 A.M., a motorcycle went through toll lane 4 without paying the toll. The motorcycle did not have any license plate.

1. The entry which should be made on line1 in the second column is  1.____
   A. 11:43 P.M.  B. 12:34 A.M.
   C. five-axle truck  D. motorcycle

2. The above passage does NOT provide the information necessary to fill in which  2.____
   of the following items?
   A. Officer  B. Date
   C. Line 1, Toll Collected  D. Line 2, Time

2 (#2)

FACT SITUATION

Peter Miller is a Correction Officer assigned to duty in Cell-block A. His superior officer is John Doakes. Miller was on duty at 1:30 P.M. on March 21 when he heard a scream for help from Cell 12. He hurried to Cell 12 and found inmate Richard Rogers stamping out a flaming book of matches. Inmate John Jones was screaming. It seems that Jones had accidentally set fire to the entire book of matches while lighting a cigarette, and he had burned his left hand. Smoking was permitted at this hour. Miller reported the incident by phone, and Jones was escorted to the dispensary where his hand was treated at 2:00 P.M. by Dr. Albert Lorillo. Dr. Lorillo determined that Jones could return to his cellblock, but that he should be released from work for four days. The doctor scheduled a re-examination for March 22. A routine investigation of the incident was made by James Lopez. Jones confirmed to this officer that the above statement of the situation was correct,

| REPORT OF INMATE INJURY | |
|---|---|
| (1) Name of Inmate | (2) Assignment |
| (3) Number | (4) Location |
| (5) Nature of Injury | (6) Date |
| (7) Details (how, when, where injury was incurred) | |
| (8) Received medical attention: date _____ time _____ | |
| (9) Treatment | |
| (10) Disposition (check one or more): <br> ____ (10-1) Return to housing area ____ (10-2) Return to duty <br> ____ (10-3) Work release ____ days ____ (10-4) Re-examine in ____ days | |
| (11) Employee reporting injury_____ | |
| (12) Employee's supervisor or superior officer_____ | |
| (13) Medical officer treating injury_____ | |
| (14) Investigating officer_____ | |
| (15) Head of institution_____ | |

3. Which of the following should be entered in Item 1?
   A. Peter Miller
   B. John Doakes
   C. Richard Rogers
   D. John Jones

4. Which of the following should be entered in Item 11?
   A. Peter Miller
   C. James Lopez
   C. Richard Rogers
   D. John Jones

5. Which of the following should be entered in Item 8?
   A. 2/21, 1:30 P.M.
   B. 2/21, 2:00 P.M.
   C. 3/21, 1:30 P.M.
   D. 3/21, 2:00 P.M.

6. For Item 10, which of the following should be checked?
   A. 10-4 only
   B. 10-1 and 10-4
   C. 10-1, 10-3, and 10-4
   D. 10-2, 10-4, and 10-4

7. Of the following items, which one CANNOT be filled in on the basis of the information given in the Fact Situation? Item
   A. 12    B. 13    C. 14    D. 15

7.____

Questions 8-11.

DIRECTIONS: Questions 8 through 11 are to be answered on the basis of the Fact Situation and the Traffic Control Report form below. Read the Fact Situation carefully, and examine the blank report form. The questions ask how the report form should be filled in based on the information given in the Fact Situation.

FACT SITUATION

Mary Fields is a Traffic Control Agent. Her City Employee Number is Z90019. She is assigned to duty at the intersection of Silver Street and Amber Avenue. On the morning of May 15, she arrives at this intersection at 9:00 A.M. and sees that there is a new *patch job* on the surface of Amber Avenue in the middle of the pedestrian crosswalk and near the northwest corner of the intersection. They day before, an emergency crew was digging here. The hole is now closed and resurfaced, but the patch job on the surface was not done very well. The patch is nearly an inch higher than the surrounding surface, and it has a sharp edge that pedestrians are likely to trip on. Mary Fields thinks this condition is dangerous, and she reports it on the Traffic Control Report form.

---

TRAFFIC CONTROL REPORT
DEFECTIVE EQUIPMENT OR UNSAFE CONDITION

1. Date of observation _____ 2. Time_____
3. Exact location_____
4. Type of equipment or condition found to be defective or unsafe_____
5. Type of defect_____
6. Name of reporting Agent_____
7. Employee No._____ 8. Precinct No._____

---

8. Which of the following should be entered in Blank 3?
   A. Silver Street at Amber Avenue, near northwest corner
   B. Silver Street at Amber Avenue, near northwest corner
   C. Amber Avenue at Silver Street, near northeast corner
   D. Amber Avenue at Silver Street, near northwest corner

8.____

9. Which of the following should be entered in Blank 4?
   A. Pedestrian traffic signals
   B. Pedestrian crosswalk markings
   C. Surface patch
   C. Unsafe condition

9.____

10. The information called for in Blank 5 is needed to determine what kind of repairs must be made and what kind of repair crew must be sent.
    Which of the following entries for Blank 5 will be MOST useful to the people who receive this report in deciding what kind of repair crew to assign to the job?
    A. Pedestrians may stumble and fall.
    B. New patch is higher than rest of surface.
    C. Emergency crew dug a hole here.
    D. Street repairs were not done very well.

    10._____

11. There is one blank on the form for which the Fact Situation does not provide the information needed.
    The blank that CANNOT be filled out on the basis of the information given is Blank
    A. 2   B. 6   C. 7   D. 8

    11._____

Questions 12-15.

DIRECTIONS: Questions 12 through 15 are to be answered on the basis of the Fact Situation and the Report of Arrest form below. Questions ask how the report form should be filled in based on the information given in the Fact Situation.

## FACT SITUATION

Jesse Stein is a special officer (security officer) who is assigned to a welfare center at 435 East Smythe Street, Brooklyn. He was on duty there Thursday morning, February 1. At 10:30 A.M., a client named Jo Ann Jones, 40 years old, arrived with her 10-year-old son Peter. Another client, Mary Alice Wiell, 45 years old, immediately began to insult Mrs Jones. When Mrs. Jones told her to go away, Mrs. Wiell pulled out a long knife. The special officer (security officer) intervened and requested Mrs. Wiell to drop the knife. She would not, and he had to use necessary force to disarm her. He arrested her on charges of disorderly conduct, harassment, and possession of a dangerous weapon. Mrs. Wiell lives at 118 Healy Street, Brooklyn, Apartment 4F, and she is unemployed. The reason for her aggressive behavior is not known.

| REPORT OF ARREST | |
|---|---|
|  |  |
| (01) _____ (Prisoner's surname)(first)(initial) | (08) _____ (Precinct) |
| (02) _____ (Address) | (09) _____ (Date of Arrest – Month, Day) |
| (03) _____ (04) _____ (05) _____ (Date of Birth)    (Age)    (Sex) | (10) _____ (Time of arrest) |
| (06) _____ (07) _____ (Occupation)    (Where employed) | (11) _____ (Place of arrest) |
| (12) _____ (Specific offenses) | |
| (13) _____ (Arresting officer) | (14) _____ (14) Officer's No.) |

12. What entry should be made in Blank 01?  12.____
    A. Jo Ann Jones        B. Jones, Jo Ann
    C. Mary Wiell          D. Wiell, Mary A.

13. Which of the following should be entered in Blank 04?  13.____
    A. 40    B. 40's    C. 45    D. Middle-aged

14. Which of the following should be entered in Blank 09?  14.____
    A. Wednesday, February 1, 10:30 A.M.
    B. February 1
    C. Thursday morning, February 2
    D. Morning, February 4

15. Of the following, which would be the BEST entry to make in Blank 11?  15.____
    A. Really Street Welfare Center    B. Brooklyn
    C. 435 e. Smythe St., Brooklyn     D. 118 Heally St., Apt. 4F

# KEY (CORRECT ANSWERS)

| | | | | | |
|---|---|---|---|---|---|
| 1. | C | 6. | C | 11. | D |
| 2. | B | 7. | D | 12. | D |
| 3. | D | 8. | D | 13. | C |
| 4. | A | 9. | C | 14. | B |
| 5. | D | 10. | B | 15. | C |

# PREPARING WRITTEN MATERIAL
# EXAMINATION SECTION
# TEST 1

Questions 1-15.

DIRECTIONS:  For each of Questions 1 through 15, select from the options given below the MOST applicable choice, and mark your answer accordingly.
  A. The sentence is correct.
  B. The sentence contains a spelling error only.
  C. The sentence contains an English grammar error only.
  D. The sentence contains both a spelling error and an English grammar error.

1. He is a very dependible person whom we expect will be an asset to this division.   1.____

2. An investigator often finds it necessary to be very diplomatic when conducting an interview.   2.____

3. Accurate detail is especially important if court action results from an investigation.   3.____

4. The report was signed by him and I since we conducted the investigation jointly.   4.____

5. Upon receipt of the complaint, an inquiry was begun.   5.____

6. An employee has to organize his time so that he can handle his workload efficiantly.   6.____

7. It was not apparent that anyone was living at the address given by the client.   7.____

8. According to regulations, there is to be at least three attempts made to locate the client.   8.____

9. Neither the inmate nor the correction officer was willing to sign a formal statement.   9.____

10. It is our opinion that one of the persons interviewed were lying.   10.____

11. We interviewed both clients and departmental personel in the course of this investigation.   11.____

12. It is concievable that further research might produce additional evidence.   12.____

13. There are too many occurences of this nature to ignore.   13.____

14. We cannot accede to the candidate's request.  14.____

15. The submission of overdue reports is the reason that there was a delay in completion of this investigation.  15.____

Questions 16-25.

DIRECTIONS: Each of Questions 16 through 25 may be classified under one of the following four categories:
   A. Faulty because of incorrect grammar or sentence structure.
   B. Faulty because of incorrect punctuation.
   C. Faulty because of incorrect spelling.
   D. Correct

Examine each sentence carefully to determine under which of the above four options it is best classified. Then, in the space at the right, write the letter preceding the option which is the BEST of the four suggested above. Each incorrect sentence contains but one type of error. Consider a sentence to be correct if it contains none of the types of errors mentioned, even though there may be other correct ways of expressing the same thought.

16. Although the department's supply of scratch pads and stationary have diminished considerably, the allotment for our division has not been reduced.  16.____

17. You have not told us whom you wish to designate as your secretary.  17.____

18. Upon reading the minutes of the last meeting, the new proposal was taken up for consideration.  18.____

19. Before beginning the discussion, we locked the door as a precautionery measure.  19.____

20. The supervisor remarked, "Only those clerks, who perform routine work, are permitted to take a rest period."  20.____

21. Not only will this duplicating machine make accurate copies, but it will also produce a quantity of work equal to fifteen transcribing typists.  21.____

22. "Mr. Jones," said the supervisor, "we regret our inability to grant you an extention of your leave of absence.  22.____

23. Although the employees find the work monotonous and fatigueing, they rarely complain.  23.____

24. We completed the tabulation of the receipts on time despite the fact that Miss Smith our fastest operator was absent for over a week.  24.____

25. The reaction of the employees who attended the meeting, as well as the reaction of those who did not attend, indicates clearly that the schedule is satisfactory to everyone concerned.

25._____

## KEY (CORRECT ANSWERS)

| | | | | |
|---|---|---|---|---|
| 1. | D | | 11. | B |
| 2. | A | | 12. | B |
| 3. | A | | 13. | B |
| 4. | C | | 14. | A |
| 5. | A | | 15. | C |
| | | | | |
| 6. | B | | 16. | A |
| 7. | B | | 17. | D |
| 8. | C | | 18. | A |
| 9. | A | | 19. | C |
| 10. | C | | 20. | B |

21. A
22. C
23. C
24. B
25. D

# TEST 2

Questions 1-15.

DIRECTIONS: Questions 1 through 15 consist of two sentences. Some are correct according to ordinary formal English usage. Others are incorrect because they contain errors in English usage, spelling, or punctuation. Consider a sentence correct if it contains no errors in English usage, spelling, or punctuation, even if there may be other ways of writing the sentence correctly. Mark your answer:
    A. If only sentence I is correct.
    B. If only sentence II is correct.
    C. If sentences 1 and II are correct.
    D. If neither sentence I nor II is correct.

1. I. The influence of recruitment efficiency upon administrative standards is readily apparant.
   II. Rapid and accurate thinking are an essential quality of the police officer.

2. I. The administrator of a police department is constantly confronted by the demands of subordinates for increased personnel in their respective units.
   II. Since a chief executive must work within well-defined fiscal limits, he must weigh the relative importance of various requests.

3. I. The two men whom the police arrested for a parking violation were wanted for robbery in three states.
   II. Strong executive control from the top to the bottom of the enterprise is one of the basic principals of police administration.

4. I. When he gave testimony unfavorable to the defendant loyalty seemed to mean very little.
   II. Having run off the road while passing a car, the patrolman gave the driver a traffic ticket.

5. I. The judge ruled that the defendant's conversation with his doctor was a privileged communication.
   II. The importance of our training program is widely recognized; however, fiscal difficulties limit the program's effectiveness.

6. I. Despite an increase in patrol coverage, there were less arrests for crimes against property this year.
   II. The investigators could hardly have expected greater cooperation from the public.

7. I. Neither the patrolman nor the witness could identify the defendant as the driver of the car.
   II. Each of the officers in the class received their certificates at the completion of the course.

8.  I. The new commander made it clear that those kind of procedures would no longer be permitted.
    II. Giving some weight to performance records is more advisable than making promotions solely on the basis of test scores.

9.  I. A deputy sheriff must ascertain whether the debtor, has any property.
    II. A good deputy sheriff does not cause histerical excitement when he executes a process.

10. I. Having learned that he has been assigned a judgment debtor, the deputy sheriff should call upon him.
    II. The deputy sheriff may seize and remove property without requiring a bond.

11. I. If legal procedures are not observed, the resulting contract is not enforseable.
    II. If the directions from the creditor's attorney are not in writing, the deputy sheriff should request a letter of instructions from the attorney.

12. I. The deputy sheriff may confer with the defendant and enter this defendants' place of business.
    II. A deputy sheriff must ascertain from the creditor's attorney whether the debtor has any property against which he may proceede.

13. I. The sheriff has a right to do whatever is necessary for the purpose of executing the order of the court.
    II. The written order of the court gives the sheriff general authority and he is governed in his acts by a very simple principal.

14. I. Either the patrolman or his sergeant are always ready to help the public.
    II. The sergeant asked the patrolman when he would finish the report.

15. I. The injured man could not hardly talk.
    II. Every officer had ought to had in their reports on time.

Questions 16-26.

DIRECTIONS: For each of the sentences given below, numbered 16 through 25, select from the following choices the MOST correct choice and print your choice in the space at the right. Select as your answer:
A. If the statement contains an unnecessary word or expression
B. If the statement contains a slang term or expression ordinarily not acceptable in government report writing.
C. If the statement contains an old-fashioned word or expression, where a concrete, plain term would be more useful.
D. If the statement contains no major faults.

16. Every one of us should try harder.

17. Yours of the first instant has been received.

3 (#2)

18. We will have to do a real snow job on him.  18._____
19. I shall contact him next Thursday.  19._____
20. None of us were invited to the meeting with the community.  20._____
21. We got this here job to do.  21._____
22. She could not help but see the mistake in the checkbook.  22._____
23. Don't bug the Director about the report.  23._____
24. I beg to inform you that your letter has been received.  24._____
25. This project is all screwed up.  25._____

# KEY (CORRECT ANSWERS)

1. D  
2. C  
3. A  
4. D  
5. B  

6. B  
7. A  
8. D  
9. D  
10. C  

11. B  
12. D  
13. A  
14. D  
15. D  

16. D  
17. C  
18. B  
19. D  
20. D  

21. B  
22. D  
23. B  
24. C  
25. B

# TEST 3

DIRECTIONS: Questions 1 through 25 are sentences taken from reports. Some are correct according to ordinary English usage. Others are incorrect because they contain errors in English usage, spelling, or punctuation. Consider a sentence correct if it contains no errors in English usage, spelling, or punctuation, even if there may be other ways of writing the sentence correctly. Mark your answer:
- A. If only sentence I is correct
- B. If only sentence II is correct
- C. If sentences I and II are correct
- D. If neither sentence I nor II is correct

1. 
   I. The Neighborhood Police Team Commander and Team Patrolmen are encouraged to give to the public the widest possible verbal and written disemination of information regarding the existence and purposes of the program.
   II. The police must be vitally interelated with every segment of the public they serve.

2. 
   I. If social gambling, prostitution, and other vices are to be prohibited, the law makers should provide the manpower and method for enforcement.
   II. In addition to checking on possible crime locations such as hallways, roofs yards and other similar locations, Team Patrolmen are encouraged to make known their presence to members of the community.

3. 
   I. The Neighborhood Police Team Commander is authorized to secure, the cooperation of local publications, as well as public and private agencies, to further the goals of the program.
   II. Recruitment from social minorities is essential to effective police work among minorities and meaningful relations with them.

4. 
   I. The Neighborhood Police Team Commander and his men have the responsibility for providing patrol service within the sector territory on a twenty-four hour basis.
   II. While the patrolman was walking his beat at midnight he noticed that the clothing stores' door was partly open.

5. 
   I. Authority is granted to the Neighborhood Police Team to device tactics for coping with the crime in the sector.
   II. Before leaving the scene of the accident, the patrolman drew a map showing the positions of the automobiles and indicated the time of the accident as 10 M. in the morning.

6. 
   I. The Neighborhood Police Team Commander and his men must be kept apprised of conditions effecting their sector.
   II. Clear, continuous communication with every segment of the public served based on the realization of mutual need and founded on trust and confidence is the basis for effective law enforcement.

7.  I. The irony is that the police are blamed for the laws they enforce when they are doing their duty.
    II. The Neighborhood Police Team Commander is authorized to prepare and distribute literature with pertinent information telling the public whom to contact for assistance.

    7._____

8.  I. The day is not far distant when major parts of the entire police compliment will need extensive college training or degrees.
    II. Although driving under the influence of alcohol is a specific charge in making arrests, drunkenness is basically a health and social problem.

    8._____

9.  I. If a deputy sheriff finds that property he has to attach is located on a ship, he should notify his supervisor.
    II. Any contract that tends to interfere with the administration of justice is illegal.

    9._____

10. I. A mandate or official order of the court to the sheriff or other officer directs it to take into possession property of the judgment debtor.
    II. Tenancies from month-to-month, week-to-week, and sometimes year-to-year are termenable.

    10._____

11. I. A civil arrest is an arrest pursuant to an order issued by a court in civil litigation.
    II. In a criminal arrest, a defendant is arrested for a crime he is alleged to have committed.

    11._____

12. I. Having taken a defendant into custody, there is a complete restraint of personal liberty.
    II. Actual force is unnecessary when a deputy sheriff makes an arrest.

    12._____

13. I. When a husband breaches a separation agreement by failing to supply to the wife the amount of money to be paid to her periodically under the agreement, the same legal steps may be taken to enforce his compliance as in any other breach of contract.
    II. Having obtained the writ of attachment, the plaintiff is then in the advantageous position of selling the very property that has been held for him by the sheriff while he was obtaining a judgment.

    13._____

14. I. Being locked in his desk, the investigator felt sure that the records would be safe.
    II. The reason why the witness changed his statement was because he had been threatened.

    14._____

15. I. The investigation had just began then an important witness disappeared.
    II. The check that had been missing was located and returned to its owner, Harry Morgan, a resident of Suffolk County, New York.

    15._____

16. I. A supervisor will find that the establishment of standard procedures enables his staff to work more efficiently.
    II. An investigator hadn't ought to give any recommendations in his report if he is in doubt.

    16.____

17. I. Neither the investigator nor his supervisor is ready to interview the witness.
    II. Interviewing has been and always will be an important asset in investigation.

    17.____

18. I. One of the investigator's reports has been forwarded to the wrong person.
    II. The investigator stated that he was not familiar with those kind of cases.

    18.____

19. I. Approaching the victim of the assault, two large bruises were noticed by me.
    II. The prisoner was arrested for assault, resisting arrest, and use of a deadly weapon.

    19.____

20. I. A copy of the orders, which had been prepared by the captain, was given to each patrolman.
    II. It's always necessary to inform an arrested person of his constitutional rights before asking him any questions.

    20.____

21. I. To prevent further bleeding, I applied a tourniquet to the wound.
    II. John Rano a senior officer was on duty at the time of the accident.

    21.____

22. I. Limiting the term "property" to tangible property, in the criminal mischief setting, accords with prior case law holding that only tangible property came within the purview of the offense of malicious mischief.
    II. Thus, a person who intentionally destroys the property of another, but under an honest belief that he has title to such property, cannot be convicted of criminal mischief under the Revised Penal Law.

    22.____

23. I. Very early in it's history, New York enacted statutes from time to time punishing, either as a felony or as a misdemeanor, malicious injuries to various kinds of property: piers, boos, dams, bridges, etc.
    II. The application of the statute is necessarily restricted to trespassory takings with larcenous intent: namely with intent permanently or virtually permanently to "appropriate" property or "deprive" the owner of its use.

    23.____

24. I. Since the former Penal Law did not define the instruments of forgery in a general fashion, its crime of forgery was held to be narrower than the common law offense in this respect and to embrace only those instruments explicitly specified in the substantive provisions.
    II. After entering the barn through an open door for the purpose of stealing, it was closed by the defendants.

    24.____

25. I. The use of fire or explosives to destroy tangible property is proscribed by the criminal mischief provisions of the Revised Penal Law.
    II. The defendant's taking of a taxicab for the immediate purpose of affecting his escape did not constitute grand larceny.

25.____

## KEY (CORRECT ANSWERS)

1. D
2. D
3. B
4. A
5. D

6. D
7. C
8. D
9. C
10. D

11. C
12. B
13. C
14. D
15. B

16. A
17. C
18. A
19. B
20. C

21. A
22. C
23. B
24. A
25. A

# TEST 4

Questions 1-4.

DIRECTIONS: Each of the two sentences in Questions 1 through 4 may be correct or may contain errors in punctuation, capitalization, or grammar. Mark your answer:
- A. If there is an error only in sentence I
- B. If there is an error only in sentence II
- C. If there is an error in both sentences I and II
- D. If both sentences are correct.

1. I. It is very annoying to have a pencil sharpener, which is not in working order.
   II. Patrolman Blake checked the door of Joe's Restaurant and found that the lock has been jammed.

2. I. When you are studying a good textbook is important.
   II. He said he would divide the money equally between you and me.

3. I. Since he went on the city council a year ago, one of his primary concerns has been safety in the streets.
   II. After waiting in the doorway for about 15 minutes, a black sedan appeared.

Questions 4-8.

DIRECTIONS: Each of the sentences in Questions 4 through 8 may be classified under one of the following four categories:
- A. Faulty because of incorrect grammar
- B. Faulty because of incorrect punctuation
- C. Faulty because of incorrect capitalization or incorrect spelling
- D. Correct

Examine each sentence carefully to determine under which of the above four options it is BEST classified. Then, in the space at the right, print the capitalized letter preceding the option which is the BEST of the four suggested above. Each faulty sentence contains but one type of error. Consider a sentence to be correct if it contains none of the types of errors mentioned, even though there may be other correct ways of expressing the same thought.

4. They told both he and I that the prisoner had escaped.

5. Any superior officer, who, disregards the just complaints of his subordinates, is remiss in the performance of his duty.

6. Only those members of the national organization who resided in the Middle west attended the conference in Chicago.

7. We told him to give the investigation assignment to whoever was available.

8. Please do not disappoint and embarass us by not appearing in court.

Questions 9-13

DIRECTIONS: Each of Questions 9 through 13 consists of three sentences lettered A, B, and C. In each of these questions, one of the sentences may contain an error in grammar, sentence structure, or punctuation, or all three sentences may be correct. If one of the sentence in a question contains an error in grammar, sentence structure, or punctuation, print in the space at the right the capital letter preceding the sentence which contains the error. If all three sentences are correct, print the letter D.

9. A. Mr. Smith appears to be less competent than I in performing these duties.
   B. The supervisor spoke to the employee, who had made the error, but did not reprimand him.
   C. When he found the book lying on the table, he immediately notified the owner.

9.____

10. A. Being locked in the desk, we were certain that the papers would not be taken.
    B. It wasn't I who dictated the telegram; I believe it was Eleanor.
    C. You should interview whoever comes to the office today.

10.____

11. A. The clerk was instructed to set the machine on the table before summoning the manager.
    B. He said that he was not familiar with those kind of activities.
    C. A box of pencils, in addition to erasers and blotters, was included in the shipment of supplies.

11.____

12. A. The supervisor remarked, "Assigning an employee to the proper type of work is not always easy."
    B. The employer found that each of the applicants were qualified to perform the duties of the position.
    C. Any competent student is permitted to take this course if he obtains the consent of the instructor.

12.____

13. A. The prize was awarded to the employee whom the judges believed to be most deserving.
    B. Since the instructor believes his book is the better of the two, he is recommending it for use in the school.
    C. It was obvious to the employees that the completion of the task by the scheduled date would require their working overtime.

13.____

Questions 14-20.

DIRECTIONS: In answering Questions 14 through 20, choose the sentence which is BEST from the point of view of English usage suitable for a business report.

14. A. The client's receiving of public assistance checks at two different addresses were disclosed by the investigation.
    B. The investigation disclosed that the client was receiving public assistance checks at two different addresses.
    C. The client was found out by the investigation to be receiving public assistance checks at two different addresses.
    D. The client has been receiving public assistance checks at two different addresses, disclosed the investigation.

14.____

15. A. The investigation of complaints are usually handled by this unit, which deals with internal security problems in the department.
    B. This unit deals with internal security problems in the department usually investigating complaints.
    C. Investigating complaints is this unit's job, being that it handles internal security problems in the department.
    D. This unit deals with internal security problems in the department and usually investigates complaints.

15.____

16. A. The delay in completing this investigation was caused by difficulty in obtaining the required documents from the candidate.
    B. Because of difficulty in obtaining the required documents from the candidate is the reason that there was a delay in completing this investigation.
    C. Having had difficulty in obtaining the required documents from the candidate, there was a delay in completing this investigation.
    D. Difficulty in obtaining the required documents from the candidate had the affect of delaying the completion of this investigation.

16.____

17. A. This report, together with documents supporting our recommendation, are being submitted for your approval.
    B. Documents supporting our recommendation is being submitted with the report for your approval.
    C. This report, together with documents supporting our recommendation, is being submitted for your approval.
    D. The report and documents supporting our recommendation is being submitted for your approval.

17.____

18. A. The chairman himself, rather than his aides, has reviewed the report.
    B. The chairman himself, rather than his aides, have reviewed the report.
    C. The chairmen, not the aide, has reviewed the report.
    D. The aide, not the chairmen, have reviewed the report.

18.____

19. A. Various proposals were submitted but the decision is not been made.
    B. Various proposals has been submitted but the decision has not been made.
    C. Various proposals were submitted but the decision is not been made.
    D. Various proposals have been submitted but the decision has not been made.

20. A. Everyone were rewarded for his successful attempt.
    B. They were successful in their attempts and each of them was rewarded.
    C. Each of them are rewarded for their successful attempts.
    D. The reward for their successful attempts were made to each of them.

21. The following is a paragraph from a request for departmental recognition consisting of five numbered sentences submitted to a Captain for review. These sentences may or may not have errors in spelling, grammar, and punctuation:
    (1) The officers observed the subject Mills surreptitiously remove a wallet from the woman's handbag and entered his automobile. (2) As they approached Mills, he looked in their direction and drove away. (3) The officers pursued in their car. (4) Mills executed a series of complicated manuvers to evade the pursuing officers. (5) At the corner of Broome and Elizabeth Streets, Mills stopped the car, got out, raised his hands and surrendered to the officers.
    Which one of the following BEST classifies the above with regard to spelling, grammar, and punctuation?
    A. 1, 2, and 3 are correct, but 4 and 5 have errors.
    B. 2, 3, and 5 are correct, but 1 and 4 have errors.
    C. 3, 4, and 5 are correct, but 1 and 2 have errors.
    D. 1, 2, 3, and 5 are correct, but 4 has errors.

22. The one of the following sentences which is grammatically PREFERABLE to the others is:
    A. Our engineers will go over your blueprints so that you may have no problems in construction.
    B. For a long time he had been arguing that we, not he, are to blame for the confusion.
    C. I worked on his automobile for two hours and still cannot find out what is wrong with it.
    D. Accustomed to all kinds of hardships, fatigue seldom bothers veteran policemen.

23. The MOST accurate of the following sentences is:
    A. The commisioner, as well as his deputy and various bureau heads, were present.
    B. A new organization of employers and employees have been formed.
    C. One or the other of these men have been selected.
    D. The number of pages in the book is enough to discourage a reader.

24. The MOST accurate of the following sentences is:
    A. Between you and me, I think he is the better man.
    B. He was believed to be me.
    C. Is it us that you wish to see?
    D. The winners are him and her.

24._____

---

## KEY (CORRECT ANSWERS)

| | | | | |
|---|---|---|---|---|
| 1. | C | | 11. | B |
| 2. | A | | 12. | B |
| 3. | C | | 13. | D |
| 4. | A | | 14. | B |
| 5. | B | | 15. | D |
| | | | | |
| 6. | C | | 16. | A |
| 7. | D | | 17. | C |
| 8. | C | | 18. | A |
| 9. | B | | 19. | D |
| 10. | A | | 20. | B |

21. B
22. A
23. D
24. A

# PREPARING WRITTEN MATERIAL

# PARAGRAPH REARRANGEMENT
## COMMENTARY

The sentences that follow are in scrambled order. You are to rearrange them in proper order and indicate the letter choice containing the correct answer at the space at the right.

Each group of sentences in this section is actually a paragraph presented in scrambled order. Each sentence in the group has a place in that paragraph; no sentence is to be left out. You are to read each group of sentences and decide upon the best order in which to put the sentences so as to form a well-organized paragraph.

The questions in this section measure the ability to solve a problem when all the facts relevant to its solution are not given.

More specifically, certain positions of responsibility and authority require the employee to discover connection between events sometimes, apparently, unrelated. In order to do this, the employee will find it necessary to correctly infer that unspecified events have probably occurred or are likely to occur. This ability becomes especially important when action must be taken on incomplete information.

Accordingly, these questions require competitors to choose among several suggested alternatives, each of which presents a different sequential arrangement of the events. Competitors must choose the MOST logical of the suggested sequences.

In order to do so, they may be required to draw on general knowledge to infer missing concepts or events that are essential to sequencing the given events. Competitors should be careful to infer only what is essential to the sequence. The plausibility of the wrong alternatives will always require the inclusion of unlikely events or of additional chains of events which are NOT essential to sequencing the given events.

It's very important to remember that you are looking for the best of the four possible choices, and that the best choice of all may not even be one of the answers you're given to choose from.

There is no one right way to solve these problems. Many people have found it helpful to first write out the order of the sentences, as they would have arranged them, on their scrap paper before looking at the possible answers. If their optimum answer is there, this can save them some time. If it isn't, this method can still give insight into solving the problem. Others find it most helpful to just go through each of the possible choices, contrasting each as they go along. You should use whatever method feels comfortable and works for you.

While most of these types of questions are not that difficult, we've added a higher percentage of the difficult type, just to give you more practice. Usually there are only one or two questions on this section that contain such subtle distinctions that you're unable to answer confidently. And you then may find yourself stuck deciding between two possible choices, neither of which you're sure about.

# EXAMINATION SECTION
## TEST 1

DIRECTIONS: Each question consists of several sentences which can be arranged in a logical sequence. For each question, select the choice which places the numbered sentences in the MOST logical sequence. *PRINT THE LETTER OF THE CORRECT ANSWER IN THE SPACE AT THE RIGHT.*

1. 
   I. A body was found in the woods.
   II. A man proclaimed innocence.
   III. The owner of a gun was located.
   IV. A gun was traced.
   V. The owner of a gun was questioned.
   The CORRECT answer is:
   A. IV, III, V, II, I
   B. II, I, IV, III, V
   C. I, IV, III, V, II
   D. I, III, V, II, IV
   E. I, II, IV, III, V

   1.____

2. 
   I. A man is in a hunting accident.
   II. A man fell down a flight of steps.
   III. A man lost his vision in one eye,
   IV. A man broke his leg.
   V. A man had to walk with a cane.
   The CORRECT answer is:
   A. II, IV, V, I, III
   B. IV, V, I, III, II
   C. III, I, IV, V, II
   D. I, III, V, II, IV
   E. I, III, II, IV, V

   2.____

3. 
   I. A man is offered a new job.
   II. A woman is offered a new job.
   III. A man works as a waiter.
   IV. A woman works as a waitress.
   V. A woman gives notice.
   The CORRECT answer is:
   A. IV, II, V, III, I
   B. IV, II, V, I, III
   C. II, IV, V, III, I
   D. III, I, IV, II, V
   E. IV, III, II, V, I

   3.____

4. 
   I. A train let the station late.
   II. A man was late for work.
   III. A man lost his job.
   IV. Many people complained because the train was late.
   V. There was a traffic jam.
   The CORRECT answer is:
   A. V, II, I, IV, III
   B. V, I, IV, II, III
   C. V, I, II, IV, III
   D. I, V, IV, II, III
   E. II, I, IV, V, III

   4.____

147

5.
   I. The burden of proof as to each issue is determined before trial and remains upon the same party throughout the trial.
   II. The jury is at liberty to believe one witness' testimony as against a number of contradictory witnesses.
   III. In a civil case, the party bearing the burden of proof is required to prove his contention by a fair preponderance of the evidence.
   IV. However, it must be noted that a fair preponderance of evidence does not necessarily mean a greater number of witnesses.
   V. The burden of proof is the burden which rests upon one of the parties to an action to persuade the trier of the facts, generally the jury, that a proposition he asserts is true.
   VI. If the evidence is equally balanced, or if it leaves the jury in such doubt as to be unable to decide the controversy either way, judgment must be given against the party upon whom the burden of proof rests.
   The CORRECT answer is:
   A. III, II, V, IV, I, VI
   B. I, II, VI, V, III, IV
   C. III, IV, V, I, II, VI
   D. V, I, III, VI, IV, II
   E. I, V, III, VI, IV, II

6.
   I. If a parent is without assets and is unemployed, he cannot be convicted of the crime of non-support of a child.
   II. The term *sufficient ability* has been held to mean sufficient financial ability.
   III. It does not matter if his unemployment is by choice or unavoidable circumstances.
   IV. If he fails to take any steps at all, he may be liable to prosecution for endangering the welfare of a child.
   V. Under the penal law, a parent is responsible for the support of his minor child only if the parent is of *sufficient ability*.
   VI. An indigent parent may meet his obligation by borrowing money or by seeking aid under the provisions of the Social Welfare Law.
   The CORRECT answer is:
   A. VI, I, V, III, II, IV
   B. I, III, V, II, IV, VI
   C. V, II, I, III, VI, IV
   D. I, VI, IV, V, II, III
   E. II, V, I, III, VI, IV

7.
   I. Consider, for example, the case of a rabble rouser who urges a group of twenty people to go out and break the windows of a nearby factory.
   II. Therefore, the law fills the indicated gap with the crime of *inciting to riot*.
   III. A person is considered guilty of inciting to riot when he urges ten or more persons to engage in tumultuous and violent conduct of a kind likely to create public alarm.
   IV. However, if he has not obtained the cooperation of at least four people, he cannot be charged with unlawful assembly.
   V. The charge of inciting to riot was added to the law to cover types of conduct which cannot be classified as either the crime of *riot* or the crime of *unlawful assembly*.
   VI. If he acquires the acquiescence of at least four of them, he is guilty of unlawful assembly even if the project does not materialize.
   The CORRECT answer is:
   A. III, V, I, VI, IV, II
   B. V, I, IV, VI, II, III
   C. III, IV, I, V, II, VI
   D. V, I, IV, VI, III, II
   E. V, III, I, VI, IV, II

8.  I. If, however, the rebuttal evidence presents an issue of credibility, it is for the jury to determine whether the presumption has, in fact, been destroyed.
    II. Once sufficient evidence to the contrary is introduced, the presumption disappears from the trial.
    III. The effect of a presumption is to place the burden upon the adversary to come forward with evidence to rebut the presumption.
    IV. When a presumption is overcome and ceases to exist in the case, the fact or facts which gave rise to the presumption still remain.
    V. Whether a presumption has been overcome is ordinarily a question for the court.
    VI. Such information may furnish a basis for a logical inference.
    The CORRECT answer is:
    A. IV, VI, II, V, I, III
    B. III, II, V, I, IV, VI
    C. V, III, VI, IV, II, I
    D. V, IV, I, II, VI, III
    E. II, III, V, I, IV, VI

8.____

9.  I. An executive may answer a letter by writing his reply on the face of the letter itself instead of having a return letter typed.
    II. This procedure is efficient because it saves the executive's time, the typist's time, and saves office file space.
    III. Copying machines are used in small offices as well as large offices to save time and money in making brief replies to business letters.
    IV. A copy is made on a copying machine to go into the company files, while the original is mailed back to the sender.
    The CORRECT answer is:
    A. I, II, IV, III
    B. I, IV, II, III
    C. III, I, IV, II
    D. III, IV, II, I

9.____

10. I. Most organizations favor one of the types but always include the others to a lesser degree.
    II. However, we can detect a definite trend toward greater use of symbolic control.
    III. We suggest that our local police agencies are today primarily utilizing material control.
    IV. Control can be classified into three types: physical, material, and symbolic.
    The CORRECT answer is:
    A. IV, II, III, I
    B. II, I, IV, III
    C. III, IV, II, I
    D. IV, I, III, II

10.____

11. I. Project residents had first claim to this use, followed by surrounding neighborhood children.
    II. By contrast, recreation space within the project's interior was found to be used more often by both groups.
    III. Studies of the use of project grounds in many cities showed grounds left open for public use were neglected and unused, both by residents and by members of the surrounding community.
    IV. Project residents had clearly laid claim to the play spaces, setting up and enforcing unwritten rules for use.
    V. Each group, by experience, found their activities easily disrupted by other groups, and their claim to the use of space for recreation difficult to enforce.

11.____

The CORRECT answer is:
A. IV, V, I, II, III  B. V, II, IV, III, I
C. I, IV, III, II, V  D. III, V, II, IV, I

12. I. They do not consider the problems correctable within the existing subsidy formula and social policy of accepting all eligible applicants regardless of social behavior.
    II. A recent survey, however, indicated that tenants believe these problems correctable by local housing authorities and management within the existing financial formula.
    III. Many of the problems and complaints concerning public housing management and design have created resentment between the tenant and the landlord.
    IV. This same survey indicated that administrators and managers do not agree with the tenants.
    The CORRECT answer is:
    A. II, I, III, IV   B. I, III, IV, II   C. III, II, IV, I   D. IV, II, I, III

13. I. In single-family residences, there is usually enough distance between tenants to prevent occupants from annoying one another.
    II. For example, a certain small percentage of tenant families has one or more members addicted to alcohol.
    III. While managers believe in the right of individuals to live as they choose, the manager becomes concerned when the pattern of living jeopardizes others' rights.
    IV. Still others turn night into day, staging lusty entertainments which carry on into the hours when most tenants are trying to sleep.
    V. In apartment buildings, however, tenants live so closely together that any misbehavior can result in unpleasant living conditions.
    VI. Other families engage in violent argument.
    The CORRECT answer is:
    A. III, II, V, IV, VI, I   B. I, V, II, VI, IV, III
    C. II, V, IV, I, III, VI   D. IV, II, V, VI, III, I

14. I. Congress made the commitment explicit in the Housing Act of 194, establishing as a national goal the realization of a *decent home and suitable environment for every American family*.
    II. The result has been that the goal of decent home and suitable environment is still as far distant as ever for the disadvantaged urban family.
    III. In spite of this action by Congress, federal housing programs have continued to be fragmented and grossly underfunded.
    IV. The passage of the National Housing Act signaled a few federal commitment to provide housing for the nation's citizens.
    The CORRECT answer is:
    A. I, IV, III, II   B. IV, I, III, II   C. IV, I, II, III   D. II, IV, I, III

15. I. The greater expense does not necessarily involve *exploitation*, but it is often perceived as exploitative and unfair by those who are aware of the price differences involved, but unaware of operating costs.
    II. Ghetto residents believe they are *exploited* by local merchants, and evidence substantiates some of these beliefs.
    III. However, stores in low-income areas were more likely to be small independents, which could not achieve the economies available to supermarket chains and were, therefore, more likely to charge higher prices, and the customers were more likely to buy smaller-sized packages which are more expensive per unit of measure.
    IV. A study conducted in one city showed that distinctly higher prices were charged for goods sold in ghetto stores in other areas.
    The CORRECT answer is:
    A. IV, II, I, III    B. IV, I, III, II    C. II, IV, III, I    D. II, III, IV, I

15.____

## KEY (CORRECT ANSWERS)

| | | | | | |
|---|---|---|---|---|---|
| 1. | C | 6. | C | 11. | D |
| 2. | E | 7. | A | 12. | C |
| 3. | B | 8. | B | 13. | B |
| 4. | B | 9. | C | 14. | B |
| 5. | D | 10. | D | 15. | C |

www.ingramcontent.com/pod-product-compliance
Lightning Source LLC
Chambersburg PA
CBHW081821300426
44116CB00014B/2443